FAMILY TIME

Family Time

The Book of the Course

LINDSAY AND MARK MELLUISH

KINGSWAY PUBLICATIONS
EASTBOURNE

ISBN 1 84291 099 X

Published by
KINGSWAY COMMUNICATIONS LTD
Lottbridge Drove, Eastbourne BN23 6NT, England.
Email: books@kingsway.co.uk

Book design and production for the publishers by
Bookprint Creative Services, P.O. Box 827, BN21 3YJ, England.
Printed in Great Britain.

Contents

Preface

Welcome to Family Time! What you will find within these pages is based on a set of talks which we have put together as a parenting course and which we teach in our church, St Paul's, in Ealing. The course has also been run very successfully in a number of other churches and schools in Britain and abroad. The course, and therefore this book, is aimed at those with children under twelve.

It was suggested to us that we should put the talks together in the form of a book so that the material could be made more widely available. You may want to read this as just that: a book from which to draw resources and information to help you in your parenting. However, should you wish to use this material to help you run a parenting course, that would be even better. We have found that parents receive a great deal of encouragement and envisioning when they meet together to hear the material and then chew it over in the course of a group discussion. One of the main benefits of doing it like this is that you meet people who are in the same situation as you are, and who are experiencing the same frustrations and joys. There is also a chance for ongoing support and friendship even after the course has finished. With this aim in mind, you will find at the back of the book an appendix entitled 'How to Run a Family Time Course' (see page 203). Also, you will find at the end of each chapter suggested discussion questions and/or suggestions about what people can do at home between chapters.

We want to acknowledge that in the course of the 13 years or so that we have been parents, we have gleaned insight from a wide variety of resources and people, much of which we have used in putting this material together. Where this is the case, we have given due credit, but if there is anything that we have remembered and rewritten unconsciously, we ask forgiveness.

We do not go into the specific area of children with special needs, because we do not feel equipped to do so. Nonetheless, many of the parents who have completed our courses have had children with special needs and have said that the material is as helpful for parenting those children as others.

We would like to thank our wonderful church family at St Paul's for all their support, encouragement and input as we put together this material. We especially thank Andrew and Nicola Holden for all their help as we have led the courses together, and the many friends who have been through the manuscript and offered their comments and ideas for improvement. Thank you also to Helen Mahood for her wonderful illustrations. We feel so privileged to be part of this church family with so much energy and enthusiasm for God and his ways.

We also want to thank our parents for all they have given us and put into our own lives. And we want to thank especially our five children, Jess, George, Callum, Beth and Josiah (without whom we could never have written such a book), for allowing us to use examples taken from our own family life and for bringing us so much joy and generally being such stars!

Mark and Lindsay Melluish

Foreword

Someone once said, 'Before I was married I had six theories about bringing up children. Now I have six children and no theories.' Parenting is not for cowards. And writing about it, while your children are still maturing, is something only the very brave or very committed will undertake. Mark and Lindsay Melluish are both brave and committed. They are brave to expose their own practices, both the helpful things and the difficulties, to a wider audience. And they are committed in that they are passionate for the future of families in our nation.

Parenting is a skill. Few are trained for it in any way apart from their own experience of being parented. As more adults carry the scars of dysfunctional family backgrounds into their own marriages, the need for training in parenting is becoming more apparent. Our government's consideration of introducing parenting classes into schools is a sign of the recognition of this need. This book is a significant contribution to meeting that.

Mark and Lindsay speak from their thinking and their experience. Many of us have been very haphazard in the ways we have developed our parenting skills, and intuitive in the way we have responded to family 'situations'. If it is true in business that 'to fail to plan is to plan to fail', it is probably also true in terms of raising our children with godly values. Mark and Lindsay believe that parenting is too important for that. They have thought and read carefully about good and bad parenting practices, and have sought to plan their family life in such a way that they enjoy their God-given role of parenting, and that their children grow up with secure emotional, moral, and spiritual foundations laid in their lives.

This book is full of useful practical tips based on what has worked and what has not in their own family. Obviously not everyone will identify completely with their life situation. Lindsay has chosen not to seek paid employment so that she can invest everything possible in her children while they are young. Many mothers are not able to make this choice about paid employment but still choose to make the family a priority, which is what this book is all about. Guarding 'prime time' together; giving each child individual attention; helping each child to learn how to express their emotions healthily and how to communicate; disciplining wisely, appropriately and fairly; maximizing helpful influences, and minimizing harmful ones: all these take time and skill, but all are based on the choice of making our families our priority. Some readers will be able to put all their recommendations into practice in their own life situation, but don't be put off if you can't. Beginning with some of the good seeds scattered throughout this book will help you prepare for the harvest that every parent longs for – a harvest of healthy children.

Many will benefit from this book. Moreover I hope that many churches will use the course not just for their own church members but for anyone in their community wanting to improve their parenting skills and family life. Parenting is a role that God gives to people regardless of whether or not they have any Christian faith. This book does not presuppose that faith. All true wisdom is from God, and helpful to believer, seeker and agnostic alike. *Family Time* is full of the universally applicable wisdom of God.

Of course the proof of the pudding is in the eating. From all I know and have seen of the Melluish family, the ingredients that they have put into their family life have begun to produce the fruit they have longed and prayed for. They would be the first to say that in the end they have to trust God, both to overcome their inadequacies as parents and to lead their children into the future he has prepared for them.

When you have finished reading this book, and doing the course too perhaps, I am sure that you will want to thank God afresh for your children, and for his grace in helping you with your God-given role as parents. And you will probably want to thank Mark and Lindsay too, and look forward, like me, to the next instalment on 'raising teenagers'!

John Coles

Introduction

It is always with a certain amount of caution that anyone attempts to write a book on parenting. We are no different. After all, we all have our ways of doing things, and who are we to suggest a different approach to parenting?

We are also excited, however, because we believe that we do have something to share. I am sure that you, like us, have been through periods of frustration and tension in your family – and have perhaps noticed other families for whom everything seems to run so smoothly and everyone seems so relaxed. Perhaps you have wondered what it takes to get from where you are now to where you would like to be.

We want to encourage you to aim for that place, and we hope you will take from this book some keys to help you get there. What we will share with you is birthed out of experience and research. We have sought to discover the wisdom of others who have written and spoken on parenting, and we hope that some of that wisdom will be valuable to you in your situation, just as it has been to us in ours. Our desire is to enthuse and envision those who want to be better parents. We certainly do not hold ourselves up as experts. We have made many mistakes along the way and there will be many more yet, we are sure. So why have we written a book on parenting?

We met as teenagers through our church youth group. From fairly early on we had an inkling that one day we would get married, so we began to dream of how things might be when we did – where we might live, how many children we might have and so on. Mark is one of four and Lindsay one of three, so it felt very normal to think that we would one day have at least three children, maybe more.

Time moved on. We finally married in our early twenties and after a few years decided that now was the time to start a family. It took some time to conceive, but after a while we had our first child, a lovely daughter. When she reached a year or so, we felt inclined to try for a second child – a two-year gap seemed to be what many of our friends were going for. After some months, however, the hopes of a two-year gap disappeared and we began to wonder whether we would have any gap at all, because nothing happened. We waited for several months without success and eventually we were advised to have some tests. The results showed that Lindsay's Fallopian tubes had somehow become blocked and the chances of conceiving again were therefore nonexistent, bar very expensive micro-surgery (which was not guaranteed to work) or a miracle.

The prospect of having no more children sent us into a time of intense emotion, during which we cried and prayed, felt angry and let down. It seemed to us that our world had caved in, and we were not sure how to cope with it. Probably we did not cope very well in comparison with others known to us in a similar situation, who managed to remain calm and faithful throughout. But we are human – and we felt extraordinarily human at that time.

A short while after receiving our bad news, a friend turned up on our doorstep announcing that he had been away on holiday in Greece, where he had had a dream about us and felt that we were in some sort of trouble. We explained about the pain of not being able to have more children and the turmoil that we were going through. He counselled us to seek every bit of medical help we could, but also said he believed God could open up Fallopian tubes. After that he prayed for us, and then he left.

We continued to pray each day for Lindsay's healing, and decided to go away for a holiday to try to sort ourselves out. We spent this time putting everything right with God and with each other. We came home exhausted, but much more at peace.

It was about two months later that we discovered Lindsay was pregnant with our second child, and he was born seven months after that. We were completely amazed that God would do that for us, and all the more so when we found we were able to have more children subsequently. Since our experience, we have set our hearts on praying for couples to conceive and could tell you many stories of people who, through prayer, have seen God miraculously enable conception to take place.

As well as that, however, our experience has made us incredibly grateful for our children – the children we had dreamed of but thought we would never have. Barely a day goes by when we do not thank God for giving them to us. It is for that reason that we felt inclined to look further into the whole subject of parenting. We felt that God had given us these special gifts, and we wanted to take care of them as best we possibly could. We read books and listened to tapes, and generally researched as much as we could – for ourselves. When we had done that, we thought that perhaps we ought to do a bit more with all the information, so we put it together in a course, and now in this book.

As we said, we are not experts. We are very ordinary. But we are passionate about family life, and what we want is for others to be passionate about it too. So we urge you to read on, and we hope that as you do so you will become as excited about your family as we are about ours.

1

A Vision for the Family

What has happened to parenting?

Parenting varies tremendously according to cultural differences throughout the world and we are aware that we only have one perspective – that of raising children in the West, where many things are available and on hand to help us. Yet even here parenting has gone through some fairly major changes in the last 30 years or so. Some of these changes are for the better, but some are for the worse.

The general demise of local communities has meant that, whereas families used to live in close proximity for generations and so helped each other in the bringing up of babies and the disciplining of children, this does not happen anymore. It used to be that parenting skills were passed down, mistakes were learned from and new discoveries were shared. These communities are now rare in the West. House prices, movement of industry and changes in the infrastructure and our educational system mean that we are all on the move. Many people leave home at 18 to go off to college; others leave in search of employment, and so the breakdown of communities spreads.

This means that we often have to discover how to parent with little or no assistance. In fact we found, when we had our first child, that it was from friends who lived close by that we learned the most. What do you do when the baby will not sleep? When do you start feeding solids? What is the best bedtime? How do you apply for schools? When do you start giving pocket money? How much do you give? How do you prepare them for leaving home and going to college? These are some of the questions that parents ask each other.

Many of us just assume that we will know what to do when the baby comes along. We will know when the baby needs feeding, we will know how to feed her and what to feed her, and of course we will soon work out the sleep issue with which we see so many others struggling! After all, we can work the Internet, use mobile phones and hold conferences throughout the world by telephone. Surely we can manage to care for a baby?

The reality, however, is that it does not always feel as easy as we initially thought it would. A friend said to us just recently that it was when her child reached two that she suddenly came to the conclusion that she needed some help – some direction to help her do the best she possibly could. We related very much to that, because that was exactly how we felt when we started out. We wanted to do the best we could for our family, but we were not sure how.

Leading the family

When we first discovered that we were expecting a baby we were very excited. Since it had taken us a while to conceive, we felt we were particularly ready for what lay ahead. What surprised us was the mix of reactions from other people. Many were as excited as we were. Others, though, had reactions we were not expecting: 'Let's hope you get an easy one,' or, 'Just you wait until they're two or three,' or, 'It's OK when they're young, but wait till they hit the teenage years.' In hindsight, we know that they meant these things kindly, but at the time it left us more with a sense of 'What have we let ourselves in for?' rather than a feeling of 'This is going to be one fantastic adventure!'

In this book we hope to encourage you and remind you that family life *is* an enormous privilege and can be fun and exciting. As well as practical pointers, we hope to give you a vision for leading your family in the direction you want to go, under God. More than ever, our families need us to lead them today. In the past families were able – far more than they are now – to rely on role models in the community to teach children the principles that govern life. We cannot expect that in our present culture, so more than ever our families need *us*, Mum and Dad, to lead them.

It is important to say here that 'family' will mean something different to each person. For some it will mean Mum and Dad and their children; for some it will be Mum or Dad parenting the children alone; for others it may mean Mum and Dad with children and grandparents or an aunt or uncle; for others still it may mean a mum and her children coming together with a dad and his children. So as we talk about 'family', please apply what we say to your own situation, whatever that is.

Chart the course before the ship sets sail

I (Mark) have always admired those ocean liners that sail across the Atlantic. The ship sets sail and when it leaves harbour the captain knows that heading out to sea will mean the ship going in approximately the right direction. However, to arrive at the right harbour at the end of the journey, the captain has to plot a course. He knows where he is going and makes sure that he does not get blown off course.

That is an apt picture of family life. It is very easy to head out into family life without knowing which way we are going. To a great extent that is what we did ourselves. But how much better to have a destination in mind and to feel secure in where we are heading. To have a goal in mind for our families makes a big difference to how things progress. I am sure that you, like us, will have started dreaming when you discovered that your first child was on the way. You may have asked yourself, 'What's family life going to be like, and how is it going to work out?' The same things are said all around the world: 'We'll do it differently from our friends,' or, 'We won't make the same mistakes our parents made.' Those thoughts are good and helpful, because what we are doing is developing a vision for our own family. The vision is what we hope for our family; how we hope our family will grow up.

It is all about the destination of our family. Where are we heading? If we can give our family a destination, we can protect ourselves, to some extent, from getting caught up in everyday management and losing sight of the vision and goal we originally had when our children started coming along. If we are not protected in this way, we may move from vision to survival. We may find ourselves seeking to survive the sleepless nights, the temper tantrums, the struggle with schoolwork, the difficulties with friends, the teenage years and the ongoing relationships, rather than thinking that this is a process through which we are working in order to get to our end destination.

Family values

That end destination will shape the values we have in our family, and those values will shape the way in which we work as a family in the here and now. They will give our family its individual feel – its DNA, if you like. The destination and resulting values will prevent us as a family from being blown off course and away from our end objective. For example, if one of your family values is to take time to be together and you find that work is demanding more and more of your time, it is very easy to be blown off course. Perhaps Dad is having to stay late at work and is not getting home in time to see the children. It happens to all of us from time to time, but it does not have to mean that as a family you no longer get together. It just means that you need to find creative ways of making up the time. Rather than losing it, you look for other ways of redeeming the time you need to be together. So you might decide to clear a space at the weekend which is normally taken up with something else, but which, equally, can give way just until work becomes less demanding again.

As we set in place values for our family, however old our children may be, if they know and share those values, those values will always remain. Just because society changes, it does not mean that our values have to change. Whatever trends of society come and go, the family values of love, kindness, gentleness, humility, patience, respect and forgiveness need never change.

There is a lovely story in the Bible (in Luke 15) of a son who went off, probably in his teenage years, and spent his father's inheritance and got into all sorts of trouble. But there was something inside him that still wanted home. When he was in trouble, it was home that he went to, because he knew that he would find the value of forgiveness there. He knew that his father would take him back. If he had not known that value, he may not have returned. We all get it wrong, but it is never too late to make a fresh start and get back on track again.

So ask yourself: what is the DNA of my family? It is all about the feel of your family and the way in which your family is made up: the atmosphere at home, the relationships between various family members, the depth and maturity of those relationships, the quality of your family time together, how meals operate, how the family communicates (the things you say to each other, what you talk about), and whether you are a family that is outward-looking and seeking in any way to make a difference in society.

Then ask yourself: what is my vision or dream of family life? What is the picture I have of family life as I would wish it to be? What do I most want for my children?

**Take a few moments to think about your
hopes and dreams for your family.**

Dream dreams for your family

How long does it take for dreams to come true? Rarely do our dreams come true overnight. It helps to have the long term in mind.

Nothing worth having comes easily.

We have all had times when we have, in desperation, gone for the quick option in order to solve an immediate crisis in dealing with our children. We may have resorted to one of the following:

- The *authoritarian* option – 'Do as I say, not as I do.'
- The *permissive* option – 'I'm worn out with it all, so I'll ignore what they're doing and hope they grow out of it.'
- The *bribery* option – 'Clean your room, and I'll treat you to an ice cream.'
- The *emotional blackmail* option – 'I won't love you if you do that.'

- The *punishment-driven* option – 'If you don't stop that I'll . . .' (In other words, we seek control through threat of punishment rather than using punishment as a corrective measure.)

While these options are all effective in the short term, in our heart of hearts we know that they may not bring the long-term results we hope for. Parenting is all about relationship, about passing on values and understanding to the next generation. It takes time.

In his book *The Seven Habits of Highly Effective Families*, Steven Covey writes about the bamboo tree:

> After the seed for this amazing tree is planted you see nothing, absolutely nothing, for four years except for a tiny shoot coming out of a bulb. During those four years all the growth is underneath in a massive fibrous root structure that spreads deep and wide in the earth. But then in the fifth year the tree grows to eighty feet![1]

Family life is so often like that. We feel we are constantly putting in and we do not always see the growth until the very end. The results may not show until adult life. We have the opportunity to influence and shape the future of our children's lives, and that process begins at birth. What we are doing now is laying the foundation – putting into place the root structure that will provide the stability for later life.

The heart

The heart has a great deal to do with this long-term view of parenting. One of our own greatest desires as parents, and what we want to encourage you towards, is to reach our children's hearts. It is about getting to know the real person inside the skin. We do not want to focus on outward behaviour, but rather to start from inside and work out.

It is from our hearts that we are motivated to do things in life.

It says in Deuteronomy 6:6–7, 'These commandments that I give you today are to be upon your hearts. Impress them on your children.' If we can reach our children's hearts with healthy values – if we can encourage them to truly take those values on board and own them for themselves – then ultimately we will see those same values worked out in their lives. Our aim is for any outward change in behaviour to be the result of an inner change of heart.

The Bible says in Proverbs 4:23, 'Above all else, guard your heart, for it is the wellspring of life.' The heart is like a well from which all the issues of life flow. This simply means that the way a person lives is an expression of his or her heart. As parents we can so easily get caught up with behaviour, and of course changed behaviour will be one of our goals as we seek to correct our children. If we focus only on behaviour, however, we may miss the underlying reason for that behaviour and therefore fail to tune in to what is going on in their hearts.

The way our children behave – the things they say and do – reflects their hearts. One of the keys to helping our children to live peaceful and satisfied lives lies in discovering the attitudes of heart that motivate their behaviour. We can all train our children not to do certain things in robot-like ways, but how much better to help them understand the reasons *why*, so that they themselves can have hearts that are motivated to do the right thing. For example, you might have a rule in your home that the children have to tidy up all their toys before they go to bed, or keep their own rooms tidy. Such rules are great – but how much better if they choose to tidy up because they understand that to do so helps the whole family.

Of course, there will be times when children will not understand the 'why' and will just have to live with the instruction to do as Mum or Dad says. After about the age of three, however, we can begin to explain the 'whys' – the moral reasons behind the practical instructions. Obedience often becomes more attractive to a child when he understands what is going on and so is less frustrated with life.

However, the process begins with us as parents. If we are to reach our children's hearts and have such a positive impact on them, then our own hearts have to be reached as well. What we do is also an expression of what is going on inside. As you read on, you will discover that some of what we cover deals with our own lives, as well as the lives of our children.

Wise words from God's word

There is much advice for parents around at the moment – many books and courses recommending different methods of parenting. You will find that the material we have used here is largely based on what we find in the Bible, and we hope that you will be as excited as we are to discover the wisdom we can take from it.

As we said earlier, we have drawn from as many sources as possible in order to try to present the collective best, but we are amazed at how many parenting courses contain principles that can be found in the Bible. As the old saying goes, 'There is nothing new under the sun' (which, by the way, comes from the Bible – Ecclesiastes 1:9). So we will often be referring to these 'wise words from God's word'.

Some of what we say may challenge things that you have grown up to accept as normal, through your own experience either as an adult or as a child. We hope that you will be ready for that, however, because unless we look in a fresh way at our family life, even questioning some of the things we do, we may not learn new things. So we encourage you to have an open mind and to enjoy the challenges.

Why use the Bible?

It comes down to a question of relatives or absolutes. Either we have a firm foundation on which to base decisions (an absolute), or we have a life based on moving ground. Jesus told a story about the wise and foolish builders (Matthew 7:24–29). It was the wise man, he said, who built his house on the firm foundation, the foundation that had stood the test of time and was able to withstand the storms when they came. The foolish man, on the other hand, built his house on the sand, the moving ground. It may have been quick to erect, but it did not last.

We are given children as a gift from God, and into their lives we can build structures that will prepare them for life. It is our firm belief that the best teaching and value system we can give our children is the value system that God has given us in the Bible. The Bible's teaching talks of a way of life that is governed by God's guidelines. The Bible will not tell us, for example, that our children should share their toys and take turns when they are playing with other children, but it does talk about teaching our children self-control, respect and care for others. The Bible touches every area of life in some way or other, either specifically or more generally. If we use it to guide and enlighten us, it will almost certainly enhance our parenting. So how does this work out?

Some of the guidelines for life we find in the Bible are very specific, such as 'Do not steal' and 'Do not lie', and these are values that most people would want to place in their children's hearts. Some things are less specific, but can help us nonetheless. Principles such as 'Love your neighbour as yourself' leave us to work out the implications for ourselves.

It is these less specific guidelines that cause us to think things through as we seek to determine what we should encourage our children to do or not to do. Sometimes our decision will depend on the circumstances. It is not always black and white. For example, we have a telephone in our kitchen, which is just next to the room where the children often play. Generally the children can play with complete freedom to make a noise and run about. However, should we be speaking on the telephone, trying to hear the person on the other end of the line, that would change things. We would then hope that the children, seeing us on the phone, would quieten down for those few moments until we had finished our call and they could continue playing their noisy game. We could forbid them to play any noisy games at all, but that would be unnecessary. How much better to respond according to the circumstances.

The Bible, therefore, can give us both absolutes (things that are black and white) and principles (general guidelines). We can use it as a plumb line to help us determine how we should live.

Our example

Children may not be very good at listening to their elders, but they nearly always seem to find ways of imitating them.

Our influence is crucial. Statistics tell us that patterns of behaviour are often repeated in families. This is, of course, not always the case and certainly patterns of behaviour can be broken. However, we will see in our children as they grow up a reflection of our own lives. We have all heard or watched with embarrassment as our children have imitated us in public. We hear them speaking as we do. We watch them acting as we do, and responding as we do. That is a bit scary, but it also brings great opportunities.

During the first few years of our children's lives, we are the heroes. Children want to be like their parents. Nothing matters more to them than what we think. As parents we are given the joy and responsibility of being role models for our children. *We reproduce who we are, not what we say!* We must try to be the kind of people we want our children to be. This means being considerate drivers, returning things we borrow, and putting the cheese we do not want back on the cheese counter at the supermarket rather than leaving it with the toilet rolls! Our children pointed out to us once that, although we expected them to make their beds before coming downstairs for breakfast in the morning, we did not always make ours. Things had to change! The point is, if we want our children to think of others first, then we have to do the same. That can be very challenging.

It is unreasonable to expect a child to listen to your advice and ignore your example.

Of course, there are many ways in which we can help our children to be other-focused or otherly, and we will be covering this in more detail later on, but we have found that having our children do jobs that serve the whole family encourages them to think of others. Laying the table, for example, is something that a child can do for everyone in the family. This is in contrast to encouraging him to do only those jobs that benefit himself, such as making his own bed or tidying up his own toys, which, although helpful and necessary, do not encourage a heart for other people in quite the same way. It is all about the heart.

**When we train the heart of a child
we train the whole child.**

In his book called *Honest to God*, Bill Hybels says this:

> Christian parents who truly understand the goal of parenting become fully engaged in the challenge. They no longer just build businesses, they build character, value and vision into young lives. They no longer treat children as inconveniences to be handed off to anyone who will have them for $5 an hour. These parents see the season of parenting as the ultimate spiritual challenge worthy of their best efforts, most fervent prayers and largest investments of time. They search for ways to improve their skills through books, tapes, and seminars and through interacting with other parents. In short, they do anything they can to encourage authentic Christian growth in their children even though it slows down their professional advancement and slows down their pursuit of professional dreams. They know that molding a runny nosed little bandit into a God honoring difference maker is the most stretching, demanding and, ultimately, fulfilling challenge that they can face. So, they earnestly devote themselves to it.[2]

As you read this book you will come across ideas that challenge, as well as basic principles and skills that every parent needs, and new horizons to reach for. We do not hope to provide for every eventuality, but we do promise you an adventure that is exciting, rewarding and fun.

Taking it further

1. Think about the hopes and dreams that you have for your family at this stage.
2. Try providing the reason *why* when you ask your child to do something (if you do not do this already), and note the response.
3. Try to consider the circumstances before making parenting decisions this week. See how it helps you in your parenting.
4. In the light of what you have just read, review the example that you set to your children now, or, if your children are very young (or they have not arrived yet), think about the example you hope to set in the future.

2

Love and Marriage

The family is the primary social unit of our society, indeed of every society, and it is one worth protecting and keeping. For relationships to grow, the people involved in them need to spend time together. For family relationships to grow, those families need to spend time together. Without time together, families become fragmented.

For so many of us, life is lived at such a frenetic pace that we do not realize how time with our families is being squeezed out – until it strikes us one day that the quality of our family life is not what we had hoped for when we first set out. We find ourselves asking, 'What happened? Has something gone wrong?'

Perhaps one of the most important areas to focus on in terms of strengthening our family units is that of the relationship between Mum and Dad. We believe that the primary place out of which grows confidence, security and hope in our children's lives is marriage.

A word to you if you are parenting on your own...

We are aware that you may be a single parent, and we want

to say that we know some of the struggles you go through. We want to take our hats off to you and encourage you as much as we can, because your job is doubly difficult and you need twice the patience, wisdom and energy. We know that you are working hard to put food on the table and create the right atmosphere for your children. We want to be behind you, and this is one of the areas where the church family can come in and support you.

In our church we have a group called SP3 – St Paul's Single Parents' Support Group. It is a place for single parents to meet regularly and support and encourage each other. Often the single mums will host an event and ask other families in the church to come, so that dads can play with all the children and provide role models for those whose dads are not often around. This group has been a great support for many of the single parents in our church and we hope very much that wherever you are, if you are parenting alone, you will be able to find similar support. We know how much you need it in your special role as a mum or dad.

Mum and Dad's relationship

We believe that, where possible, the primary relationship in a family is that between Mum and Dad. All other relationships depend on it and the quality of that relationship will affect the quality of all other relationships in the family. The way you treat each other will be reflected in the way other members treat each other.

The focus of this chapter is to consider the role of the marriage relationship within our families and what we can do to help keep it in good order. If you are parenting alone, however, please do not switch off. We have included some pointers for you, and we do believe that much of what we have written here will have a bearing on how you parent in your situation.

A man called Theodore Hesberg said, 'The most important thing a father can do for his children is to love their mother.' Let's look at what he meant.

Wise words from God's word

It says in Genesis 2 that God created man and then decided that it was not good for him to be alone. Man was surrounded by animals and had a wonderful relationship with God, but he was still deemed by God to be 'alone'. What he needed was an intimate relationship with one of his own kind; someone with whom he could share life intimately at every level – spiritually, socially, emotionally and physically. So God decided to 'make a suitable helper for him', a helper being someone who would complete and complement the man in every way. He created the woman and brought her to the man, and united the two: 'For this reason a man will leave his father and mother and be united to his wife, and they will become one flesh' (verse 24).

So we see that God's purpose for marriage and in creating woman was to provide a companion for man – someone with whom he could share his life. We were meant to be together. In the creation story, it seems that God saw the coming together of the woman with the man as his ultimate achievement, because once he had completed the process and seen that it was 'very good', he rested (Genesis 1:27–31).

It is interesting to note that, even though they had no children as yet (they came along later), God looked upon the coming together of the man and woman as 'very good'. This is significant for us because it conveys the message that a man and woman who are married to one another are complete. They do not have to wait for an allotted number of children before being considered a complete family. As husband and wife they are already complete. When children arrive, their family increases in size, but the children do not make them any more of a family.

How does all this affect us now?

This means that, even though we have children, our relationship with our partner is the most important relationship in the family. The quality of all the relationships in the family, and also the security of our children, will depend on the quality of Mum and Dad's relationship. That seems quite a challenge and a responsibility, but it does show us the importance of making our marriage the best it can possibly be – not just for our own benefit but for the sake of our children.

So often we think our children's needs should come first. We get so tied up with the children that we forget about our husband or wife, or if we do remember them it is not until the end of the day when we are exhausted and falling asleep in front of the TV. Often this is done with the best of intentions – to do the best for our children. What can happen, however, is that our relationship begins to lose its vitality and, ironically, it is the children who lose out. Nothing we can buy or do for our children is more important than showing them that Mum and Dad love and value one another and that together we lead the family.

What if you are parenting on your own?

As we have said already, we know that life can be and often is extremely hard for those who are bringing up children without the support of a partner. With several single parents as friends, we are aware of the many issues that face you on a daily basis.

You may have discovered already that your relationship with God, if you have one, makes a difference as you rely on him to help you raise the family, and this is a good and positive means of outward focus. It will also be a source of support and strength in your parenting, because God is someone who loves to listen and care. Let your children know how important your relationship with God is. Bring them to worship regularly and mix with other families. Get support from your church family. Let the children draw security from seeing you spend time with God, and allow the strength you draw from him to be a source of stability in your relationships both inside and outside the family.

Families whose lives revolve around the children

If you are like us, as soon as you had your first child you will have begun to take much more of an interest in how your friends, family and work colleagues bring up their children. You will undoubtedly have had ideas about what you saw, deciding either that it was definitely *not* how you were going to do it, or that you admired it and wanted to build some of it into your own family life.

You may have come across families for whom everything revolves around the children; where the children seem to be the focus of life itself. Of course, we are not saying that time spent with the children is not important, and in the next chapter we will be looking at the whole area of investing in our relationship with them, but we do believe that sometimes the children become so much the focus of life that other relationships begin to suffer.

When our first child was born, we were more than delighted and it seemed so normal to talk about her and focus on her all the time. So many people had said that we would no longer have time for ourselves or for each other once our children came along. Yet we know that, difficult though it may sometimes be, the best thing we can do for our children is to provide a strong marriage.

To live our lives completely centred around the children may bring problems for various reasons:

- If we allow our children always to be our priority, *our focus shifts away from our partner* and we no longer fulfil our role as husband or wife. Instead we tend to hide behind the role of Mum or Dad, where we can feel less exposed and accountable.

- If we are parenting on our own, having our child as the central focus of our life can lead to that child, as he or she gets older, taking the place of a husband or wife. In this way *the child becomes an equal and a friend to Mum or Dad* – a relationship that is difficult for a child to cope with.

- To build our lives around the life of a child can give him *the feeling that he is self-reliant* – 'I can manage on my own and I don't need anyone else.' We are not saying, of course, that a child should not be encouraged to do things for himself, but to foster a sense of not needing other people might put him at a disadvantage in the long term. Our children will benefit so much from learning that other people matter, regardless of whether they will always gain personally from maintaining a relationship with them. You may be able to think of families where the children are positively encouraged to look out for other people and to consider their feelings, even though it might not ultimately benefit the children themselves. Such children often talk easily with other adults and children, and have an ability to make those people feel valued even though they might not know them very well at all.

- If our lives revolve solely around the children we may give them *more freedom than they can cope with* – especially if this happens before they have acquired the self-control to manage such freedom. For example, we all know that to allow our two-year-old the freedom to roam around in a supermarket may be great fun for him initially, but unless he has the self-control to manage, he is likely to pull over a stack of tins or boxes and may well injure himself and cause havoc. He may think he is fine, but in fact he is in danger.

- *We may find it difficult to set boundaries for our children*, and may find ourselves having to adapt the boundaries rather than face addressing the behaviour of our child.

If a child learns that he is at the centre of the family, he may tend to be self-centred and have difficulty in making relationships both inside and outside the family unit. He will tend to be a taker and not a giver. On the other hand, a child who sees his place in the family more as a member of a team will be confident and secure about where he fits in. He will therefore make relationships naturally and comfortably, giving as well as receiving, and growing up knowing the importance of investing in family relationships and caring for others.

How can we avoid revolving our lives around the children and make Mum and Dad's relationship a priority?

- Remember, *life does not stop when you have children*. It changes, but it does not stop. Just because you become a father or mother, do not stop being a sister, brother, friend, daughter, son and, above all, a husband or wife.
- When you arrive home, *make a point of saying 'hello' to your husband or wife*. Make it a priority to do that first, before attending to the clamouring children, so that everyone knows that Mum and Dad matter to each other.

If you are parenting on your own, you could ask your family and friends, and particularly your own parents, to make a point of greeting you first when they arrive before making a fuss of the children. Explain to them that you want the children to see you valuing other close relationships as well as your relationship with them.

- Try to *take time to talk to your husband or wife every day without interruptions* – when the children are around to see, not after they are in bed! They might object at first, but soon they will grow to enjoy seeing you enjoying time with each other and will feel more secure as a result.

- *Guard your privacy* by asking the children to knock on your bedroom door before they come in.

- *If you are parenting on your own and it is your habit to pray, try doing it when the children are awake*, and let them know that this is something that is helpful for you. Once they are used to it and understand it, they may well draw security from this and look forward to your time spent with God. If this does not work for you, however, try to find another way of making sure the focus is not always on the children.

- *Do something together* as husband and wife, say, once a week. Go to the cinema, go out for a walk or a meal, have a takeaway at home with a video, play tennis. Have a weekend away once in a while. It can be anything you both enjoy, but do it together without the children and let them know why you are doing it: because you enjoy being together. Leave each other notes or text each other on your mobile phones. Let the children know that you like to keep in touch with each other. If you are parenting on your own, do the same, but with a good friend or family member. Be sure to get out and do something for yourself and with someone other than your children. Keep up your contacts outside the family.

- *Use your home to serve other people.* Entertain as a family to help each other work as a team and to help the children learn to look outwards towards the needs of other people. We often entertain over a Sunday lunchtime and sometimes we might ask the children who they think would enjoy an invitation to lunch. Having decided together who to invite, we can all take a share in entertaining those people and giving them, hopefully, a good time.

How can I learn to say, 'I love you'?

Children who are assured of their parents' love for each other will have greater confidence in their parents' love for them, and in turn this sense of being loved can enhance and strengthen other relationships. Nonetheless, in marriage and family life love is not always the easiest thing in the world! There are times when we have to *choose* to love. Love is a word that is used so much these days that it seems to have lost much of its depth of meaning. We say we love chocolate, or we love a colour, or we love that dress, but that is very different from the love we experience in family relationships.

Wise words from God's word

The Bible tells us that love is not just about feelings, but is also a choice. Paul says in Colossians 3:14, 'And over all these virtues put on love...' Notice the words 'put on'. If love were just a feeling, then we would not be able to 'put it on'. We cannot command feelings, but we can command choice – and love is a choice. We can love someone with our actions. It is not just about words. In marriage and family relationships, we would say that we choose to love and that this choice will lead to action.

Accounts for love

In his book *His Needs, Her Needs*, Willard F. Harley talks of each of us having a 'love bank'.[1] It is a bank with many different accounts in it. In fact, it has an account for each and every person we know. Each person makes either a deposit or a withdrawal every time we interact with them. Pleasurable interactions result in deposits and painful inter-actions result in withdrawals.

Harley explains that in this love bank system each deposit and each withdrawal is worth a certain number of love units. If, for example, I meet a friend and the meeting leaves me feeling comfortable and warm, then love units are deposited in that friend's account. If the meeting is great and we laugh all evening, then more units are added. However, the opposite is also true. If, after my meeting with my friend, I leave having been made to feel miserable, then love units are withdrawn from the account. As life goes on, so the accounts in our love bank fluctuate. Some build sizeable deposits, and others might just hang in there in the black. Others, however, can go overdrawn because our relationship with them causes more pain than peace.

Obviously, the love bank concept is not intended to be

mathematically accurate, but it does highlight the fact that we affect each other emotionally with almost every encounter. We want to take this concept and put it into our marriage and family relationships, because in family life we are affecting each others' 'accounts' every day.

The love languages

Another similar idea is that each of us has a love tank which is waiting to be filled with love. If that tank is constantly on empty, our marriage will be lifeless. Just as a car needs filling up with fuel to keep going, our love tanks also need filling up if we are to give the best to our partners. But why is it that so often our love tanks are on empty? Why do we sometimes not truly feel loved? One answer is that people are different, and different people speak different love languages. If you tried to tell a French person that you loved them and they did not speak English, your words would mean nothing. In the same way, your emotional love language and the language of your husband, wife or children may be as different as English is from German, French or Chinese.

John Gray writes in his book *Men are from Mars, Women are from Venus*:

> We mistakenly assume that if our partners love us they will react and behave in certain ways – the ways we react and behave when we love someone. This attitude sets us up to be disappointed again and again and prevents us from the necessary time to communicate lovingly about our differences.[2]

If we are to be effective communicators of love, we must be willing to learn our partner's primary love language (or the way they most readily give and receive love). We are going to look at how this works out in practice. While we have drawn examples largely from the marriage relationship, bear in mind – especially if you are parenting on your own – that these love languages apply not only to husbands and wives but to children and close friends as well.

The Five Love Languages is a book that we highly recommend.[3] The author, Gary Chapman, outlines five basic areas through which we tend to give and receive love and explains that one or two of these areas will probably be more important to us than the others. Let's look at these five areas in more detail.

1. Words of affirmation

One way of expressing love is to use words which build up (see 1 Thessalonians 4:18 and 5:11). Some people seem to enjoy and need this encouragement more than anything else. Genuine verbal compliments or words of appreciation are powerful communicators of love. They are best expressed in simple, straightforward statements of affirmation such as, 'You look great in that dress,' or, 'Thanks for sorting out a babysitter for tonight. I really appreciate it,' or, 'The car looks great. Thanks for taking the time to clean it.' Imagine the effect on a marriage if a husband and/or wife heard those sorts of things regularly. I (Lindsay) know that I am far more motivated if I am complimented rather than criticized. I know, too, that Mark is the same.

Another way of giving affirmation is to use encouraging words. Many of us lack confidence and could achieve so much more in life if we had someone to encourage us and make us believe we can do what we want to do. So, for example, if your husband says he is thinking of going to Weight Watchers once the warmer weather arrives, you could either say, 'At last! I've been hoping you'd do that for ages!' or you could say, 'Good for you. I'm sure you'll do well because you're always so determined once you set your mind on something. Maybe I could do it with you and we could change what we eat to suit your diet. We'll probably both feel better for it.' Words like this might not come easily at first, but it is worth persevering. I (Lindsay) know that I have achieved so much more in life because Mark has been willing to encourage me. What a great gift to give to a husband or wife who responds to words of encouragement!

Words of affirmation can also be kind words. If someone is ranting and raving at you and you choose to respond lovingly with kind, gentle words, you will know how the heat can be taken out of the situation. A while ago, I was in the post office and inadvertently went up to a counter that was closed. The clerk was rather irritated with me and made it clear by pointing to the 'closed' sign. I felt so awkward that I apologized not just once, but intermittently throughout my dealings with him. By the end he had completely changed his attitude and assured me that it had been no trouble and it was not my fault at all. There is a proverb in the Bible that says, 'A gentle answer turns away wrath' (Proverbs 15:1). Once the anger has passed, we can seek to discover what the problem was in the first place.

Another way of speaking words of affirmation is to make requests humbly, rather than make demands. 'You know that fruitcake you sometimes make? Would it be possible to have one this weekend? I love that cake!' This is a great way of offering affirmation as well as letting your partner know gently what you like and showing him or her how to love you.

So, if your husband or wife responds to words of affirmation, make a conscious effort to accumulate things you can say to affirm him or her. And try praising your partner to others. If it filters back to your loved one, it will give him or her a huge boost!

2. Quality time

Some people need time to be given to them more than anything else in their special relationships. They love to spend time with their husband or wife, either doing something together – a sport, or a hobby, or having a meal in a restaurant – or simply having a good conversation, sharing openly, listening to one another and really communicating. For some people, time like this really builds them up and, as a result, puts deposits in the love bank of their husband or wife who has given them that time.

Quality time means giving someone your undivided attention. That means not sitting with half an eye on the football as your wife tells you how hurt she was this evening that you failed to notice her new hairstyle – but rather sitting on the sofa with the TV off, talking; or going for a walk together; or going out for a meal together. The key word is 'together'. For some it might not have to involve talking. Quality time might be just playing tennis together, for example, or going shopping, visiting an antiques fair, or having a picnic. And the great thing about these outings and activities is that they also provide a memory bank to draw from in the years ahead.

For most people whose primary love language is quality time, however, talking will be important. Your wife, for example, may want to know that loving her by giving her quality time and conversation will mean that you will listen sympathetically to what she has to say and respond by asking the sorts of questions which show you have understood her. A lady came to us some while back and said that her husband was wonderful in so many ways, so helpful around the home, always tidying up and doing the odd jobs that were needed. 'But,' she said, 'if only he would read about these Love Languages he might realize that he is completely missing the point when it comes to what makes me feel loved. I just long for quality time with him.'

I (Mark) know that Lindsay is not a television fan. She rarely switches it on unless there is a certain film or programme that she particularly wants to watch. On the other hand, I will often come in from a busy evening out and turn on the TV to help me unwind. Generally I hope to catch the news, but I will also see if there is anything else worth watching for half an hour or so. The problem is that I get totally engrossed in whatever is on. Lindsay will come and sit with me and will often want to talk about the day rather than watch TV. I have learned that if I want to give her quality time at that moment, I have to choose to turn off the TV in order to ensure that the time we have really is 'quality'.

If you are not really a quality time person, but your partner is, there are certain things you can learn: to listen; to maintain eye contact when your spouse is talking; to listen for feelings; to watch body language; and not to interrupt. You might also need to learn to share your own feelings. If your wife 'wishes you would talk more', she is looking for intimacy in conversation and that involves revealing yourself as well as listening. If your partner's primary love language is quality time, and specifically conversation, her emotional love tank will never be filled until you share with her your thoughts and feelings. This might not come easily to you, especially if you grew up in the kind of home where feelings were not shared, or if you have a strong, silent personality and you are married to a chatterbox! But it will be worth it.

3. Gifts

For some people, to receive a gift from a special person when it is not connected to a birthday or Christmas means more than anything. A gift is a visual symbol of the fact that someone remembered you when you were not there. It does not have to be expensive, but just the fact of being given it makes you feel loved and appreciated.

These tangible symbols of love are more important to some people than to others. Those who are likely to feel loved through receiving a gift often tend to give gifts to other people. When we first got married, I (Lindsay) would sometimes go off shopping on a Saturday afternoon either by myself or with a girlfriend. While I was out, I would tend to buy a little something for Mark, and more often than not it would be a pair of socks. I would present this gift to him with great glee, but unbeknown to me, he had no idea why I kept buying him socks when he already had a drawer-full upstairs in the bedroom! We both realize now that what I was doing was expressing my love to him, but unfortunately I was doing it in a way that meant very little to him. He is not really a gifts person. Often we show love to others in the way we would like to have it shown to us.

4. Acts of service

Love is a choice. When we choose to do something for our partner or our children that we know they would like us to do, we are showing them love in action. The Bible talks about loving 'with actions and in truth' (1 John 3:18), and it also says, 'Serve one another in love' (Galatians 5:13).

We all have specific roles in the home (emptying the kitchen bin, vacuuming the car, and so on), and it really makes a difference to some people if their husband or wife helps them out by doing a job which would normally not be their responsibility. It might be that you fill up your wife's car with petrol to save her doing it the next morning, or you make your husband's sandwiches because you know he has to leave very early the next day. If your partner is not a morning person, you will know that to get out of bed five minutes earlier than usual and make him or her a cup of tea or coffee will make a great difference to the start of their day. In the same way, helping by doing the vacuuming, emptying the dishwasher, hanging out the washing, cooking a meal, mowing the lawn, or anything else that is not usually your job will help to show your love in action.

In our home, it is generally my (Mark's) job to make sure that the car is cleaned. Recently Lindsay has found that she can take the car and get it cleaned quite reasonably just near to our home. For me to come home and find the car clean so that I do not have to do it myself means a great deal. That is Lindsay showing her love for me in action.

If your partner's primary love language is acts of service, their love tank will soon fill up as you show them love in action. The important thing is to do those things which you know they want you to do and to do them not because you are coerced but because you choose to.

5. Physical touch

We all know that physical touch is a way of communicating emotional love. We know that babies and children who receive plenty of hugs and kisses develop a healthier emotional life than those who are left without. We know too that physical touch is a powerful vehicle for communicating marital love. Holding hands, hugging, kissing and making love are all ways of communicating emotional love to your partner. For some people, physical touch is their primary love language. Without it they feel unloved. With it their love tank is filled and they feel secure in the love of their partner.

Men are quite different from women. In *His Needs, Her Needs*, Willard Harley lists the five chief needs of men and the five chief needs of women, taken from a survey. Neither list contains anything at all that is on the other, and it also shows that for many men physical touch is high on their list of priorities. For many men, sex is as important as quality time is for many women. Without it they do not feel loved.

Without it their love tank will never be full.

Love touches may be explicit, such as in the act of making love, or they may be implicit and require only a moment, such as a hand on the shoulder as you pour a coffee or a kiss as you pass each other in the kitchen. If you did not grow up in a tactile family, this might not come easily to you at first, but if you discover that physical touch is your partner's primary love language you can soon learn to find ways to express love.

Our children and their love languages

We parents love our children, and equally we want our children to feel that they are loved. If you can discover your child's primary love language, you will be at a distinct advantage in loving your child in a way that makes him *feel* loved as well as just knowing that you love him. When children are little, it is difficult to know what their primary love language is, so pour on all five and you are bound to be right! If you watch them carefully, however, you can discover it early.

- If your child is always making and wrapping presents for you and responds very positively when given a gift, *receiving gifts* may be his primary love language. He gives because he likes to receive. If so, gifts do not have to be expensive or cost anything at all. The fact that they are given will be enough to fill the tank.
- If your child runs to you and jumps on your lap when you arrive and strokes your hair and wants to be touched, his primary love language may be *physical touch*. If so,

give him plenty of hugs and kisses, as many as he can take.

- If your child always comes and shows you things he has written or drawn, and looks for praise or responds very positively when his behaviour is praised, then *words of affirmation* may be his primary love language. If so, give him lots of encouragement. Praise his successes rather than highlighting his failures – and this, of course, goes for all children anyway.

- All children need *quality time*, some more than others. What you can do is to enter into their interests, watch them playing sport, listen to them practising the piano, give them the time they are looking for. If you do this when they are young, the chances are that they will allow you to spend time with them in their adolescent years and beyond.

- If your child is often very grateful for the things you do for him and often offering to help you, his primary love language may be *acts of service*. Helping him to mend his bicycle or a toy will mean a lot to him and will help to fill his tank.

Going back to ourselves, how can we discover our *own* primary love language? Ask yourself these questions:

- What makes me feel most loved by my partner? What do I desire above all else?
- What does my partner do or say that hurts me? (If criticism springs to mind, maybe your love language is words of affirmation.)
- What have I most requested of my partner? The thing you

most request is probably the thing that would most make you feel loved.

- How do I most express love to my partner? Often we express love in the way we would like it expressed to us.

Why not spend a few minutes working out the order of your love languages, then try to work out the order for your partner and for your children. Enjoy the difference it makes to your family life as you seek to put love into action!

Taking it further

1. Consider this question: does your family revolve chiefly around your children, or, on the other hand, are the needs of each member of the family considered to be equally important?

2. This week, when you come home in the evening, try spending five minutes talking with your husband or wife before taking time with the children. See how your children respond.

3

When They Are Young

In Chapter 1 we introduced the idea of reaching our children's hearts so that we might enable them ultimately to live a life which brings fulfilment and contentment. We shall develop this idea as we go on, but for now we are going to look at an area which is key if we are to be at all effective in our aim. If we hope to bring up our children in such a way that they are able to take on board for themselves the good things we want to pass on to them, it is helpful if:

- our relationships with them are strong;
- channels of communication are always open;
- our children know we love them.

In this chapter, therefore, we are going to look at some practical things we can do to build relationships with our children that look to the future.

The time when we, as parents, have most influence and opportunity to shape and guide our children's lives is when they are very young – and it is a relatively short period, perhaps between ten and twelve years. How many of us have said to ourselves, 'I can't believe how quickly they're growing up'? The first thing that helps us towards our hopes and dreams is being there with our family, being present with our family. Children need our time today, and it is not just quality time they need, but quantity time.

Presence is spelt T-I-M-E.

The expression 'quality time' has become a very fashionable one in recent years. This probably has something to do with the increasingly frenetic lives that some of us live as families, which means that often time together gets squeezed out. The result is that the time we do spend together becomes all the more precious, and perhaps we call it 'quality time' in the hope that it will be just that.

It has become the thing to work on an assumption that quality is better than quantity. The 'quality time person' may not have much time, but what they do have they will make the most of. The 'quantity time person', on the other hand, thinks that just by being around, by being visible, somehow communication is happening. Yet we all know how easy it is to be around physically but not emotionally. Our physical presence does not necessarily indicate our commitment to someone. Equally, we know that just because people are talking about quality time does not mean it is a reality, and there are still many children who crave quality time even though their parents love them to bits.

A key to communicating with children is to put in a lot of quantity time so that the quality time can happen.

We watched with awe and wonder, over this last year, when someone we did not know came to live with us for a month. He phoned up to say he was coming to Ealing but had nowhere to live. As we knew his parents, we invited him to come and live with us. While he was with us, one of our boys had a competition at school to design a boat and sail it across the school swimming pool. Joel decided to take this project on with our son, and together they made a very capable boat that would sail across the pool. However, they decided that this boat was not good enough and they needed to make a bigger and better one. For that whole month, each and every night there was a conversation about this boat and neither of them lost enthusiasm or passion for it. Our son reckoned that Joel was the best person who had ever walked through our front door. Why? Because he was interested in the things that our son was interested in. He had spent time doing the things that our son wanted to do.

If we are to build an open, honest, trusting relationship with our children in which they are able to come to us with confidence whatever the problem and whatever their age, we will need to invest time, both quality and quantity.

**The best thing parents can spend on
children is time, not money.**

Reading this may make some of you feel uncomfortable. It certainly makes us feel uncomfortable at times! It may be that some of you would love to give your children more time, but you are separated from them because of family break-up. Others may have to work extremely long hours just to keep the wolf from the door. The last thing we want is to heap any guilt on your shoulders. Nonetheless, it is probably good for all of us to be reminded of the important things we should be doing with our time.

A report that recently came out from Harvard University said that the single most common factor producing anger, rage and hostility in children was the perceived inaccessibility of one or both of their parents. Our presence matters.

Here is part of an essay written by a nine-year-old, entitled 'What is a Grandma?'

> Grandmas don't have to do anything except be there. If they take us for walks they slow past things like pretty leaves and caterpillars and they never say hurry up. Usually grandmothers are fat but not too fat to tie their shoes. They wear glasses and funny underwear and they take their teeth and gums out at night. Grandmothers don't have to be clever, just be able to answer questions like why isn't God married and why do dogs chase cats? Grandmothers don't talk baby talk to us, like visitors do because they know it's hard for us to understand it. When they read to us they don't skip pages or mind if it's the same story over and over again. Everybody should have a grandmother, especially if you don't have a television because they're the only grown-ups that have time.[1]

Yes, our presence matters. Time spent with our children matters, and it matters at every age.

Take a few moments now, and think about the time you have available for your children.

What can we do to encourage communication with our children?

If you are anything like we are, you may be aware that often you are telling your children what to do while they are trying to tell you their dreams and wishes. Listen to this conversation between a father and his son over tea one evening.

'Hey, Dad, I'd really love us to go skiing. Sam goes every year. He says he's really good at it and he can go zooming down the mountain really fast. Can we go, Dad?'

'Mmm . . . that's all very well for Sam, but skiing is very expensive and we're not really that sort of family. Now hurry and eat up. I want to get you into bed so I can get to my evening meeting.'

We are sometimes so busy with our lives that the children just have to fit in. How else might that dad have responded?

'Wow, that sounds fantastic! It sounds like you'd really enjoy learning to ski, and I'm sure you'd soon be going fast like Sam. I don't know if we could go on a skiing holiday, but maybe we could try a dry slope one day, or even arrange for you to go with the school on one of their trips.'

Sometimes we make the mistake of thinking that communication is the ability to express ourselves. So we talk *to* our children rather than talking *with* them. Communication, when it works properly, is not about expressing our thoughts but about drawing out the thoughts of another person. Our object in communication with our children must surely be to understand them.

How often have we heard or been part of the sort of teatime conversation set out above? Our children have very little 'life baggage' that gets in the way of what they are thinking or saying. What they have to say is therefore very important. How can we learn to listen?

Practical tips

- Physically get down to the level of your child. Perhaps kneel or sit when he is talking.
- Look him in the eye. Show him that he has your full attention.
- Do not try to do two things at once. Listen only to your child.
- Reassure him that he has your attention by touching him on the face or arm.
- Wait for him to finish what he is saying! It may take a while, but it is worth it.

What will be the end result? Ted Tripp says this:

> Sensitive communication with your children enables them to understand the complexities of life. They learn that life is concerned with both the world of feelings and the world of ideas. It means understanding yourself and others. It means having long-term vision as well as short-term goals. It means we become concerned for more than the 'what' or 'what happened' but also about the 'why'.[2]

To communicate with your children is to invest long-term in their characters. The more you talk with your children, helping them to understand themselves, their temptations, doubts, fears and anxieties, the more you will prepare them for life in the world. You will also teach them that their thoughts are of value and that you want to understand them better because they matter so much to you.

Let's look at an example. Your child is putting on the new jumper that your mother-in-law knitted him for Christmas. You knew when he opened it on Christmas Day that he was not really pleased with it, but you had asked her to knit him a jumper and in an error of judgement you left her to choose the wool and the pattern. Now he is getting ready to go to his friend's house and he is crying. What will you do?

If your objective is to let him know your thoughts, you might say something like this:

'Look, I know you're not very pleased with that jumper, but just put it on and stop looking so miserable. There's nothing the matter with it. Granny spent a lot of time making that for you and you ought to be more grateful. It might not be the style your friends wear, but what does that matter? They don't always know what looks best. Now hurry up and get ready, or we'll miss the bus.'

On the other hand, if your primary objective is to understand what your child is going through inside, you might have a conversation like this:

'You're fed up about having to wear that jumper, aren't you?'

'Yes.'

'You knew as soon as you opened it that you didn't like it, didn't you?'

'Yes, I was really disappointed.'

'But you didn't want to say so in case you upset me?'

'No.'

'What don't you like about it?'

'It's so uncool. It looks really stupid.'

'I don't know what you mean.'

'No one wears jumpers their granny knitted. Especially not purple ones.'

'So it's the colour you don't like. And the fact that it's home-made?'

'Yes. All my friends wear fleeces. And the best ones have a logo across the front. Everyone will think I'm a big girl's blouse wearing this stupid woollen thing. They'll all laugh at me.'

'That must feel horrible.'

'Yes. It makes me think no one likes me.'

You have just got in touch with the heart of your child by communicating with him at a deeper level and hearing his inner feelings.

Just recently, one of our boys began to complain that he had no friends at school. Initially we responded, 'Of course you have!' and merrily listed the names of all the children in his class we had ever heard him talk about. After all, the teacher had told us that he was popular and always got on well with everyone in the classroom. But he continued to say that he had no friends. This went on for a few days while everyone, including his teacher and his big brother and sister, repeatedly told him that of course he had friends. Then one day it struck us that, whatever the reality might be, in his little mind he did not believe he had friends. Sometimes he was alone in the playground and this meant, to him, that he had no friends. We needed to take that seriously.

We changed our response. We began to listen more carefully to what he was saying and to show that we understood how he felt. We made suggestions about what he might do sometimes to draw his friends to him in the playground and very soon, although he still had times when he was on his own, he became his happy self again. Little had actually changed. His friends were no more his friends now than they had been all along. But because we had listened to him and he had felt understood, he believed we cared and was then in a stronger position to cope with life in the playground.

Paul Tournier said, 'It is impossible to over-emphasize the immense need humans have to be really listened to, to be taken seriously, to be understood. No one can develop freely in this world and find a full life without feeling understood by at least one person.'

Three worlds

We all have three worlds:

- Our public world, the part of us that is open for anyone to see.
- Our personal world, which is open to those close to us.
- Our private world, which we open up just every now and then to those we trust.

Children have the same three worlds, and from time to time as parents we are invited into that very private world. It may be last thing at night, just as your child is settling down to sleep, or when you are alone doing a small task together. Sometimes your child will say, 'Daddy/Mummy, do you know...' and you will find yourself invited into her private world. She is about to share something private and personal, and your response is crucial. If you tell her not to be silly or make light of what she says, then she is less likely to open up to you next time. If, on the other hand, you can be attentive and show you care, however childish the point may be, you are more likely to be invited into that private world later on in life, when things might not be quite so childish.

A young girl might be talking to her mum or dad one night and in the midst of the conversation she might suddenly say, 'Do you think I'm pretty?' The response, 'Don't be so silly, of course you are,' may reassure her to some extent – but how much better to try to get behind the question and discover where it has come from, as well as giving that much needed reassurance. The comment might have come because she has been called names at school, or because she has heard others being told they are pretty but it has not been said to her for a while. This is a precious moment and needs careful handling. An appropriate response might be this: 'Yes, darling, I do think you're pretty. I think you're beautiful! What makes you ask me that?'

Remember that communication is the art of expressing sensitively what is in your heart, and of hearing completely and understanding what another thinks or feels. *Allow your children into your world too*. Communication is a two-way thing, and if we share our heart with our children – let them know what is important to us, what our dreams and visions and hopes are – they will be far more likely to share their hearts with us.

Building relationships

Communication at a deeper level is our aim. Building relationship is the key to that aim. What can we do to build relationships with our children and ensure that they really do feel that we love them? Here are five suggestions.

1. Do things together

If we want a relationship to grow, it will mean committing to it in terms of time. If something means a lot to us, we spend time on it. Our children need us to spend time on them. With children, the best way to spend time together is to do things together – play a game, go for a walk, go swimming, do some gardening, watch a video, eat a meal. Do whatever you like, as long as you do it together.

Recently Mark was out for the evening and, as it was a Friday, I (Lindsay) suggested to our eldest daughter that she might like to stay up a little later than usual after the younger ones had gone to bed. Her eyes lit up at my suggestion, and they became even brighter when I suggested that we might play draughts together. We spent half an hour or so playing our game and chatting, and then she went happily off to bed. When I went to bed myself a couple of hours later, on the bed was a slip of paper on which my daughter had drawn a big heart. Inside she had written in large letters, 'I love you'. My guess is that the note came because of the half hour I had invested earlier in the evening. My time with her had made her feel loved in a way that words alone would probably never have done.

As we spend time with our children we find that, very often, good conversation follows – conversation of the sort we have discussed above. Making time to do things together creates an environment in which we can talk with our children about important things. It is worth remembering that our children will probably learn more from talking with Mum and Dad than we will ever realize, so let's not pass up these opportunities.

2. Encourage with words

It says in 1 Thessalonians 5:11, 'Encourage one another and build each other up.' The word 'encourage' means 'to instil courage'. In giving our children encouragement we are looking to give them the courage to go further, to enlarge their borders.

We are often very good at praising our work colleagues, our friends' children, our neighbours for their gardening skills or DIY, our friends for their new hairstyle or latest bargain – and yet we are not so good at praising those we love most. Children need to hear words that inspire and encourage them. As parents we have the power to discourage or encourage by what we say to our children. An encouraging word spoken appropriately is often the thing that determines whether a child takes on board the action or attitude for which we are offering praise.

One of our children had a party for her third birthday. Quite naturally, there were moments when one of her brothers struggled with all the attention his sister was getting! Having settled into it, however, he was able to enjoy seeing her celebrating her birthday. As we tucked both our boys into bed that night, we said, 'Well done at the party today. We were proud of the way you joined in and helped your sister to have such a good time.' The grins on their faces said it all.

So speak words of encouragement:

- 'Thank you for taking out the rubbish. That really helps me.'
- 'Well done for getting yourself dressed. You've really learned to do that quickly now.'
- 'You've worked very hard at [learning to play football/getting dressed in the morning/leaving your bedroom tidy/picking up your toys] and it's made a real difference.'

Words like this, which emphasize effort and improvement, are such motivators. We have noticed how often such words genuinely help our children to achieve their potential.

Words can be very powerful. When Cheryl Prewitt was four years old, she hung around her father's small country grocery store in America. Almost daily, the milkman would come into the store and greet her with the words, 'How's my little Miss America?' At first she giggled, but eventually she became comfortable with it. Soon the milkman's greeting became a childhood fantasy, then a teenage dream. Finally it became a goal, and in 1980 she stood on a stage in Atlantic City and was crowned Miss America. The words of that milkman had a great impact on Cheryl's life.

Words do not have to be spoken – they can be written too. We have sometimes written a note and popped it in the children's lunchbox, or left it among their schoolwork, or simply laid it on their pillow. Sometimes these written words are even more precious because they can be kept and looked at again another day.

Another important thing to remember is that we need to allow our children the freedom to fail. For a child to feel that he or she is a failure can be disheartening. To say, 'Come on, you're six years old now, you should be able to tie your own laces,' as you take over and tie the laces up for your child is very different from saying, 'You try really hard to tie your laces these days – well done. Would you like me to help you learn so that you can do them on your own?'

If our children are afraid of failing for fear of looking foolish, they may well hold back rather than stretch themselves to their full potential. They need to know that, as long as they have tried their best, failure is fine and we will always stand by them whatever happens. An encouraging parent looks for effort rather than success. Let's look for improvement and seek to encourage and inspire our children in every way possible.

If you have more than one child, it is sometimes tempting to expect them each to be good at what the others are good at – and even at what we do well ourselves. We know, however, that this is not always the case, and it is good to acknowledge that we are all different and our children are all different. That is a great thing. If one of our children is good at sport and we are also into sport, we may wish that our other child was sporty as well. But how much better to thank God that he is different and draw out of him what he is really good at. He might be very musical, for example, and you could focus on that. It is actually very freeing when siblings are good at different things. It enables them to enjoy their particular interests without competition creeping in.

3. Give plenty of hugs

Studies have shown that many parents only touch their children when it is necessary, such as when they are dressing them, putting them in the car, or taking them up to bed. Yet hugging is a very effective way of making our children feel loved. As parents, we can develop a relationship with our children that is not just verbal but physical too. This will mean hugging our children when we want to congratulate them, as well as hugging them when they are hurting. To deprive our children of physical hugs now might mean that they will have difficulty hugging us after they leave home, and yet it might well be the very thing they still need. Children of all ages and both sexes need physical expressions of love. A son needs his father's loving touch as well as his mother's, and a daughter needs plenty of physical affection from her mother as well as from her father.

Author Paul Planet says this:

> Hugging is very healthy. It helps the body's immune system. It keeps you healthier. It cures depression and reduces stress. It induces sleep. It is invigorating. It is rejuvenating. It has no unpleasant side effects. Hugging is nothing less than a miracle drug. Hugging is all natural. It is organic and naturally sweet. It contains no pesticides, preservatives or artificial ingredients and is 100% wholesome.
>
> Hugging is practically perfect. There are no moveable parts, no batteries to wear out, no periodic check-ups, no monthly payments, no insurance requirements. It offers no energy consumption and returns a high-energy yield while being inflation-proof, non-fattening, theft-proof, non-taxable, non-polluting and fully-returnable.[3]

Our example as parents will be helpful in all this. As we show our love for one another by hugging in front of our children, they will see that physical touch in a long-term, committed relationship is natural thing.

4. Keep your promises

It may seem an obvious point to make, but to build trust and communication we have to be trustworthy. 'I'll play with you later' rolls all too easily off the tongue, and, while it may solve an immediate situation, it is less than helpful in the long run. We may forget to play, but our children will not forget. If we can be trustworthy and keep our word, then our children are more likely to grow to be the same.

One day, during the school holidays, I (Lindsay) promised our son that later that day we would go out and buy the new trainers he had been needing for a while. However, as the day went on and one thing after another crowded into it, I began to realize that we were not going to be able to get out and fulfil the promise I had made. Feeling rather guilty, I hit on the idea of inviting a friend round instead. 'Would you like to have your best friend round for the afternoon?' I asked our son, who was delighted at the idea. I was pleased too, and assumed that he would realize the trainers were now out of the question for that day. The boys had a great time playing and, as I settled our son down at bedtime that night, I said, 'You really enjoyed yourself this afternoon, didn't you?' Our son replied, 'Yes . . . but Mummy, why didn't we get my trainers?' That was a question I found hard to answer.

Our memories are all too short, but our children's are not.

---

5. Tell your children regularly that you love them

All children need to be told in words that Mum and Dad love them. For some people, especially if it was never said to them when they were children, this may not come easily, but it is worth persevering and practising at every opportunity.

In our family we not only say the words out loud, but we often write them down and even sometimes use sign language to get our message across. The children love this 'secret' way of communicating our love, and it is especially fun in a crowded place such as at a school concert or when

we are saying goodbye at the school gate and do not want
our children to lose face with their friends.

And finally, a word to the dads...

An article in *The Times* (28 January 1999) said, 'Fathers
who devote time to their sons – even as little as five minutes
a day – are giving them a far greater chance to grow up as
confident adults, a parenting research project has found.' It
went on, 'Boys who feel that their fathers devote time especially to them and talk about their worries, school work and
social lives almost all emerge as motivated and optimistic
young men full of confidence and hope.'

Building boys is better than mending men.

We believe that dads play a special part in the family. Often
today, dads are away from the home for much of the time.
Yet our boys need us around as male role models, and for
the rough-and-tumble games that boys love to play. And our
girls need us to affirm their femininity. Dads have an equally
crucial role to play in family life as mums do, and we want
to encourage them to play their full part in bringing up the
children.

Our central message here is this: *build relationships with
your children while you have the chance*. When our children
are young, we – as mums and dads – are largely in control
of all they do. God made it this way because our children
have been entrusted to us and we, through our love and
care, will look after them. As they grow older, however, our
control diminishes as they begin to make their own

decisions and choices. We hope that in place of that control will come our guiding influence – but this will only be possible if we have laid firm foundations for the relationship between us and our children. We found the following diagram to be a helpful illustration of this.[4]

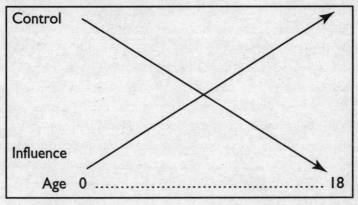

Our influence will only be as great as the effort we have put into making strong relationships. Our aim must be to build a relationship that will stand the test of time. As we spend time with our children now, building a relationship of trust, we are laying the foundations for a life of unity in the family.

Taking it further

1. Begin to work on listening and communicating in the ways the chapter has suggested, and see how your child responds.
2. Try to be aware this week of how good you are at listening to your partner or to other adults.
3. Look for opportunities to encourage and praise your children.

4

Family Time

We all remember the day our first child was born, when we were overawed by that tiny baby lying in the cot. No doubt we all thought that he or she was the most precious little child ever to be born. Within a very short time, however, we began to realize what a responsibility it was to be caring for that little baby. We began to realize that the way we treated him or her would ultimately have quite an effect on how he or she turned out.

As parents we quickly become aware that children are like sponges: they absorb what they are exposed to incredibly easily, and from day one our children are being shaped and moulded by life's circumstances and the influences around them. All the issues of family life have a profound impact on the people our children will eventually become.

Wise words from God's word

The Bible tells us that our early childhood experience has lifelong implications for us as individuals. It also sheds light on family life and on how children should be treated and brought up (see, for example, Deuteronomy 6, Ephesians 6 and Colossians 3). Much has also been written, particularly in recent years, about the bearing that our foundational years of childhood have on us as adults. This shaping is not automatic, however. Just as important as the effect of these events and circumstances is the way a child responds to them. It is this response that will determine the effect they ultimately have.

The people our children become are a product of two things:

1. *Life experience*. What is life like for our children? In what environment are they being brought up? Are both parents around and, if so, do they have a harmonious relationship?
2. *How they interact with that experience*. Our children react and respond to their circumstances, and our job as parents is to know where our children need guidance and structure to help them respond appropriately, so that they are not blown hither and thither by every wind which comes in their direction.

Over the next two chapters we are going to focus on some of the positive and negative influences which our children are under in today's world, and the effect that those influences have. In this chapter we shall look at the role of the family and the impact it has on our children. In the next chapter we shall look at outside influences and their effect, then at our children's relationship with God and the important part that this plays in determining how they respond to everything else.

The family

When our children are very young, the family is one of the major influences on them. As they grow older and start to make friends of their own, there is a tendency for this influence to diminish and what other people say becomes increasingly important. It is good to stand back from time to time and take a look at our family life. What impact is it having on our children? Are there things we need to do to strengthen it, so that it can remain a positive influence that will help to shape their future life and values, hopefully even when they hit the teenage years and beyond?

There are many aspects of family life that have a bearing on who our children become. Let's take a closer look at some of them.

1. Family structure

The structure of the family in a child's particular situation is one of the most obvious factors that will affect him or her. Is he part of a traditional nuclear family? Does she live with one parent or both parents? Are those parents available, or physically or emotionally absent? Do grandparents live nearby and play an active part in family life, or do they live at a distance? Is the child an only child, or are there siblings? What is the birth order of the children in the family? Are they close in age, ability and personality? Is there a stepparent in the home, or step-brothers and sisters? Does anyone in the family have a physical or mental disability? All these aspects should be taken into account and their likely effects considered.

2. Family roles

Within any family, the roles played by each member will vary. Some fathers are preoccupied and unavailable, others are very much involved in every aspect of family life. In some families the mother takes complete responsibility for child care, while in others it is the father who is chiefly responsible for the practical day-to-day running of the family. Children, too, have differing roles. Much is expected of some children in the home and almost nothing of others.

We need to assess what our individual roles are. It is a shaping factor in the lives of our children. Will they see Dad doing the washing up and sweeping the kitchen floor, or is it only Mum who does these things? What model are we showing to our children through our roles? If you grew up in a family where you were encouraged to do some of your own ironing and were given the freedom to cook meals and help around the house, you may well find now that it is a natural thing to pick up a tea towel or the vacuum cleaner, either at home or at someone else's house. In turn, you may find that your older children have noticed you doing that and tend to do the same.

3. Family conflict

The way problems are approached varies enormously from family to family and will have a bearing on the children's ability to face life's difficulties. Does the family know how to talk through problems in order to resolve them? Are problems swept under the carpet in order to keep the peace? One of the wise sayings in the Bible reads, 'The way of a fool seems right to him, but a wise man listens to advice. A fool shows his annoyance at once, but a prudent man over-looks an insult' (Proverbs 12:15–16). If conflict is dealt with wisely and sensitively, a child will learn that problems are better resolved than ignored. In this way, the influence of the home helps the children to think things through carefully and be wise in their decisions.

4. Family failure

We touched on this in the last chapter, where we said that if children are free to fail without being criticized or laughed at, they will grow in confidence, safe in the knowledge that even if they do make a mistake it is not the end of the world. If parents can see failed attempts as praiseworthy efforts, seeking to encourage their children, this will be a positive shaping influence in those children's lives.

5. Family history

Every family has a history, and each one is different. There are births, deaths, marriages, divorces, house moves, job moves, financial concerns, sickness, accidents, and so on. Some families have lived in the neighbourhood for genera-tions and the children have grown up with their friends and family around them. Others have moved around continually, and the children have had to make new friends and cope with new situations on a regular basis. Again, all of these considerations will have a profound effect on the lives of the children.

6. Family values

Every family has values of some sort – developed attitudes, ideas and beliefs which affect the way we operate. What is important to the parents? What is worth a fuss, and what passes without notice? Are people more important than things? Do parents get more stressed over a hole in a school jumper or a fight between schoolfriends? What philosophies and ideas does the child hear? What are the spoken and unspoken rules of family life? Where does God fit into family life? What is important in the home? We will look at this in more detail in a later chapter, but it is worth saying here that if we are to share our values with our children, then it is good to start while they are young.

Clearly, as parents we want to provide the most stable influences for our children. Some of the things we have mentioned above are already established (such as family history and family structure), so in a sense there is nothing we can do to change their effect on our children. Others, however, are very much open to change, and we are all able to look at our families and ask ourselves a few helpful questions.

- Is ours a family where our children are free to fail in the knowledge that they will always be loved unconditionally?
- Are we, as a family, offering our children a secure place in which to learn to discuss issues and resolve problems openly and sensibly?
- Are we happy with the example we set as parents in terms of the roles we have in the home?

It is never an indication of failure to see a need to make changes in family life. And it is never too late. Now is the time to be proactive in our families and to change things for the better if we feel the need.

Take a few moments now, and consider the following 'family patterns' questionnaire.

Family patterns

The most important model we have of marriage and parenting, for better or worse, is our own family. Jot down your responses to the following points and talk with your partner about how similar or different your experiences were.

In my childhood home . . .
We used to make jokes often / sometimes / rarely.
We used to touch each other frequently / sometimes / hardly ever.
Kisses and cuddles were normal / measured / rare.
When people felt angry they hit out / rowed / sulked / talked.
We would discuss our plans fully / partly / reluctantly.
My business was everybody's / interesting / my own.
We prided ourselves on our concern / interest / independence.
Nakedness was accepted / avoided / frowned upon.
Sex was discussed readily / when necessary / never.
Children were disciplined by my Dad / my Mum / both / neither.
Children said prayers with my Dad / my Mum / both / neither.
We went out together / independently / rarely.
I liked it when my Dad . . .
I liked it when my Mum . . .
I was unhappy when . . .

Today in my immediate family . . .
What my child might say they like best about my family is . . .
What I like best about my family is . . .
I can rely on my family to . . .

Something my parents did that I do not want to happen in my home is . . .

I expect to be in touch with my relatives daily / weekly / monthly / two or three times a year / as little as possible.

Family identity

We have begun, then, to look at how our families might help to shape the lives of our children in a positive way. For the remainder of this chapter we will focus on something that we believe is of great importance in determining our children's response to all our positive input – something that determines whether they ultimately hold on to what we have taught them when other influences in their lives get stronger.

Peer pressure is something that all of us are aware of, and perhaps we think that there is little we can do to lessen its influence. We believe, however, that there *is* something that can help to minimize peer pressure – and that is a strong family identity. If family identity is strong, if our children feel involved in and proud to belong to their family, they are more likely to hold to its values and principles. Children who feel uninvolved in their family and have little sense of belonging are more likely to look outside the family for a sense of identity and a set of values.

There are exceptions, but you may have noticed that young people who come from families who appear to be a strong unit often cope better in the face of temptation from friends. You may have noticed others, too, who seem to have less time or affection for their families and who willingly follow the crowd. There is great security in belonging to a group, and where family ties are weak, young people often find that security with friends.

Whether you are a couple parenting together, or a single parent caring for children on your own, there is a great deal you can do to work at building this strong sense of family identity.

1. Be a team

Being a team encourages a family to be interdependent. 'Independence' is a fashionable word at the moment, and we are encouraged to help our children to be independent from a very early age. We all love it when children can do a certain amount for themselves, but too much independence too soon may lead to a lack of family identity. Interdependence, on the other hand, encourages family unity and identity. It is amazing what strength and resources we can find within us if we encourage and are encouraged by those with whom we are working. Teams, when they work together, can achieve a great deal.

At our children's school there is a system whereby each child is put into a 'house'. Any special achievement, piece of work or act of kindness is rewarded with points which are added up at the end of term and totalled together with the points of all the other children. The winning house is announced at the end of each term, and there is always great excitement to see which team will win.

Children love to feel they are part of a team.

As mums and dads we have a special role here, and we can give the lead in being a team. We can encourage everyone and let it be known that we think our family is a great team to be part of, that everyone is important, and that we should all be looking out for each other. 'How are we doing, team?' or, 'Come on team!' are words that we can use to build up a sense of pulling together as a family. The more we can build a sense of team spirit, the more we can build a family that works and plays together, the stronger our family identity will be.

Being a team means supporting and encouraging the team members.

One summer term, we went to watch our daughter taking part in her school sports day. As we sat in the sun enjoying the day, we noticed that the girls ran not for themselves but for their parents. It was the cheering from the mums and dads that made the difference. We also noticed the girls whose parents had not been able to be there, and the way those girls were looking for support from their classmates instead.

We can be a team by:

- Entertaining together.
- Tidying up together.
- Cleaning the car together.
- Serving together to help others.
- Taking part together in a sponsored project in the community.

One summer we as a family felt it would be fun to raise some money for one of the charities that we support together

– The Toybox Charity – and the children decided that they would like to hold a small garden fête. They planned the fête together and designed a leaflet that we were able to print out on our computer and deliver to the houses around us. The whole event was very simple, with five or six tables with games on, a small bric-a-brac stall and some light refreshments. We were amazed to find that we had raised about £160! Any family could do something similar, and it is a great way not only to look outward and serve others, but also to encourage a sense of family unity.

Lessons from geese

Fact 1: As each goose flaps its wings it creates an 'uplift' for the birds that follow. By flying in a 'V' formation, the whole flock adds 71 per cent more range than would be the case if each bird were flying alone.

Lesson: People who share a common direction and sense of community can get where they are going quicker and easier, because they are travelling on the trust of one another.

Fact 2: When a goose falls out of formation, it suddenly feels the drag and resistance of flying alone. It quickly moves back into formation to take advantage of the lifting power of the bird immediately in front of it.

Lesson: If we have as much sense as a goose, we stay in formation with those headed where we want to go. We are willing to accept their help and give our help to others.

Fact 3: When the lead goose tires, it rotates back into the formation and another goose flies to the point position.

Lesson: It pays to take turns doing the hard tasks and sharing leadership. As with geese, people are interdependent on each other's skills, capabilities and unique arrangements of gifts, talents or resources.

Fact 4: The geese flying in formation honk to encourage those up front to keep up with their speed.
Lesson: We need to make sure that our honking is encouraging! In groups where encouragement is shared, productivity is much greater. Individual empowerment results from quality honking.

Fact 5: When a goose gets sick, wounded or shot down, two geese drop out of formation and follow it down to help and protect it. They stay with it until it dies or is able to fly again. Then they launch out with another formation or catch up with the flock.
Lesson: If we have as much sense as geese, we will stand by each other in difficult times as well as when we are strong.

2. Have family time

One activity that we (and many of the families with whom we have worked) have found helpful in building strong foundations and relationships in family life is what we call 'family time'. In Chapter 2 we looked at making our marriage the primary relationship in a family, and saw how the children extend the family but do not complete it. 'Family time' is simply putting this into action, with time set aside first for Mum and Dad to talk together, and then for the children to join them so that the whole family can be together and each has a chance to share and listen to everyone else.

To have a time set aside for the family at least once a week, when the purpose is to talk and listen to each other, will help to strengthen your family and will let every member know in a tangible way that family is your priority. Perhaps one will have a problem and the others can all help to sort it out. Perhaps one is rejoicing over an achievement and the others can share that gladness.

It does not matter what you call it, but a name is helpful because it means you can gather for this special time any-where, even if you are on holiday. Our children will often say to us, 'Let's have family time,' and everyone knows what that means. For us family time means that we all sit on our bed and take turns to say anything that is important to us. It may be something that has happened to us, or something we have enjoyed. It may be a difficulty we are going through and for which we need support.

What is the value of family time?

1. It is a place to bring up something that we, as parents, want to talk to the children about, perhaps something related to our life as a family that we need to change or redress. Recently, for example, we felt that we had, as a family, failed one another in the way we had been relat-ing. Too much criticism had crept in, and kind words and encouragement had not been enough of a feature. We talked a lot about it, and everyone agreed that we all like and need to hear kind words and encouragement and that we would all try to make it a priority. After that, we were back on course.

2. It is a place for the children to bring up things they want to talk about or question.

3. It is a place to teach something new or to introduce some-thing new into family life.

4. It is a place to talk about an important event that is coming up, to prepare for it together by sharing our

excitements, our fears and worries.

5. It is a place to laugh together.

6. It is a place to pray together.

Friends of ours have family time on a Friday evening because that suits their week best. It may be that you set aside 20 minutes for family time on a Sunday morning, before the day begins. There is no right or wrong time, place or way to have family time. What matters is that it works for your family.

To have family time now helps us as parents to equip our children for all walks of life. It will provide a place where our children can ask about all sorts of things, and, because we have been talking and listening to each other on a regular basis, we will always have that safe place in which to talk naturally, both now while they are young and also later on in their teenage years.

Of course, family time will not be the only time we talk with our children! Often children talk when they want to, and perhaps they will ask to have family time when we have not necessarily planned it. So we can be ready to talk at other times too. But children do love having this special slot set aside for them, and often respond well to it.

3. Set family jobs

Children who are encouraged to help often learn quickly to take on some of the responsibility of running the home. Helping around the home does not need to be seen as a chore, but rather can be an opportunity to communicate and learn together.

We have found that this creates a greater sense of family

unity, and that even the little ones can have their job to do. Children will learn if they are allowed to have a go, and in the safety of the home we can stand by to help and guide them. Below is a list of jobs that your children might do to help around the home. There will be many others that relate specifically to your family. You might like to consider which jobs your children would be able to do already, and which ones they might learn to do fairly soon.

- Set the table for a meal
- Feed pets
- Make drinks
- Make beds in the morning
- Help with cleaning
- Tidy garden of toys
- Pick up litter in garden
- Make cups of tea or coffee
- Clear up their toys after use
- Put dirty clothes in the wash basket
- Clean windows
- Wash car
- Help with washing up
- Help with ironing
- Help with the gardening
- Cook a meal

Giving our children jobs to do builds a sense of responsibility. As we trust them to wash up or to feed the pets, we encourage them to do their bit in the family. We believe, too, that those jobs which affect the whole family – such as laying the table – are very good for encouraging a sense of team spirit and a willingness later in life to muck in where help is needed.

In all of this we need to be wise. Too much responsibility too early could be overwhelming, but too little could leave the children believing that you do not trust them. It is also important to understand that by giving our children responsibility we are not washing our hands of our role and responsibility as parents. We are sharing our responsibility with them. This means that we should take care to check how they are getting on with their jobs rather than get cross when things do not happen as they should.

4. Make a family quote book

All children, and adults too, come out with hilarious and sometimes embarrassing quotes that cause many a laugh. A fun way of building that sense of being a team is to set up a family quote book. Write down some of the funnier family quotes. As the children get older, they can write in it too.

I (Mark) was driving our two boys to school recently and, because our son was a little rusty on his recorder homework, he decided to practise in the car. He was doing very well, playing through 'Old MacDonald Had a Farm', until about halfway through when he suddenly stopped and looked out of the car window. 'What are you doing, son?' I asked. 'You're only halfway through the piece.' 'No, Daddy, I'm meant to stop here,' came the reply. 'There's a rest in the music.'

In our family we often refer back to something someone said in the past and the way in which they said it. This creates a family history, and helps to build a very real sense of belonging.

5. Take family photos

Having photos around the home is another great way of recording family history and giving the family a sense of identity.

How about creating a collage at the end of the year which includes photographs of all the important events – birthdays, Christmas, weddings and so on – that have taken place during that year? You could have one for each year that your children have been alive, hung on the wall at home. This is great for the children. Children have such a limited concept of time, and yet a few photos on the wall will remind them that they were small once. It will allow them to look back at holidays and special moments. And they love to look and remind themselves of what birthday cake they had when they were two, three, four, five, and so on. It helps to keep in focus the fact that we are a family and that we do things together.

And remember to have some photos up of Mum and Dad without the children too, before they came along, or even since. It is good for everyone to see those as well.

6. Create family traditions

Do you rip open your presents at 4.30 a.m., or are you a 'we'll wait until after lunch' family on Christmas Day? These sorts of things build family traditions. There is no right or wrong way, there is simply a family way. When we got married, we soon discovered on our first Christmas that we had different family traditions. We chose to do things our own way from then on, and now we are creating more traditions as the children grow older.

It is not just at Christmas, though. We always visit a roadside restaurant on our way to our holiday destination. It was something we started, and now our children look forward to it. They know that we are going to stop for breakfast or dinner, depending on what time of day we are travelling. It has become a family tradition.

One of our sons had a birthday a while ago and he was, naturally, very excited. He came into our bedroom the day before, snuggled up to us and said, 'Tomorrow is the day when I'll come in and sit between you both and the others will be down the other end of the bed and I'll open my presents, won't I?' Neither of us had realized how the precise detail of that family ritual was so important in his little life.

Family traditions are simply another way of saying, 'This is us and this is the way we do things together.'

- Start a tradition of taking each child out for a celebratory meal when they reach the age of eleven.
- Start a tradition of having a special family trip to McDonald's or somewhere similar at the end of the school term.
- Start a tradition of having a family walk in the countryside on Bank Holiday Monday.

7. Be together

'Families who spend significant amounts of time together as a unit are also more likely to turn out confident children' is the statement made by a parenting research project called 'Tomorrow's Men', supported by Oxford University. Sadly, time together is often a low priority in many families today.

There are times when life can be so busy with after-school

activities, sports clubs, recorder lessons, piano lessons, football coaching, Cubs, Brownies and the many other things that crop up daily. It is therefore good to be creative in our family activities as well. Mealtimes can be a great opportunity for being together. Eating together builds a sense of belonging. Sometimes eating separately is necessary for convenience, but mealtimes can be a great time to talk, catch up on news and do an activity together. Sometimes work commitments make it impossible to have a family meal every day. If that is the case, make Sunday lunch special, or Friday supper – whatever fits into your family rhythm.

Do things together. Recently I (Mark) spent a few hours in the garden and made the most of the time by asking one of our sons to help me. As we worked, we talked about our family and how we were making the garden special for everyone to use. It also gave us an opportunity to laugh together, when I fell out of a tree and onto a pile of weeds, much to my son's amusement!

Here are some ideas about activities you might do together as a family.

- Go on cycle rides.
- Have a family pizza night with a good video.
- Go for walks together.
- Eat meals together as often as possible.
- Sleep in the tent together in the garden.
- Sit in church together.
- Eat ice creams together.
- Do the gardening together.
- Read a book together.

Let the children choose sometimes what they would like the whole family to do together. It does not matter what you do, as long as you all enjoy it and you do it together.

Work at having fun together and at invoking an atmosphere of fun in the house – make it a haven for happiness, a place to party and a place for children to enjoy themselves. Having fun is important. Our children need to be able to laugh at the world and at themselves to keep a balanced view of life. When children laugh and have fun it releases anxiety and fears. Often there is no fun in a family because we do not have time for fun. If we do not have time for fun, we are too busy.

Wise words from God's word

Proverbs 17:22 says this, 'A cheerful heart is good medicine, but a crushed spirit dries up the bones.' Look for ways to enjoy fun times as a family together. Laugh at some of the things that go wrong together and try to find out what makes your children laugh. Look for things that you will enjoy together as a family, and go and do them. You have to study fun, find out what it is that you as a family most enjoy, then plan for it.

Make family holidays a priority. Holidays are a must. They do not necessarily have to be expensive trips abroad to sunny places. Camping holidays are cheap and just as fun. The important thing is to get away together, away from the busyness, and have time doing fun things together and investing in family memories.

All these activities and any others you can think of become important highlights in the lives of our families.

They help to show our commitment to the family and to build trust. Our children will remember these good times, and they create precious memories for everyone to look back on.

As we close this chapter, let's ask ourselves these questions:

- Are we cultivating a sense of team spirit within our family, or is independence valued more than interdependence?
- Is our family one that our children are glad to belong to?
- Do our children feel involved in our family?

The family is an important factor in determining who our children become. We have an opportunity to invest time and energy now that will reap many rewards later in life.

Taking it further

1. Consider the structure of your family and what effect it might have on your child or children. Are there things that you would like to change and can change?
2. Consider steps you might take to strengthen the identity of your family.
3. Try having family time and see how your children respond.

5

Outside Influences

In the last chapter we considered how the family could be a very positive influence for our children, and we suggested a number of practical ideas for strengthening the family identity. As we all know, however, even if the family unit is strong, as the children get a bit older it will not be the only area of influence. In this chapter we will look at some of the other influences which are likely to affect our children.

As we have already suggested, children are like sponges and will soak up everything they are exposed to very easily and quickly. We watch our sons playing football in their branded football tops which 'all the others wear'. We listen as our children tell us what their friends have told them during the day, and see how they hold them in high regard. The feeling of 'I wish I could be like...' comes very early in life. As our children grow older and begin to have freedom to be a bit more independent, outside influences become stronger and they are going to be faced not only with positive ideas and activities but negative ones as well. As parents we can be aware of these influences, and try to equip our children to make decisions based on what is right and good.

By the age of seven, or even earlier, our children are being affected by different opinions on all sorts of subjects: sex, drugs, music, the environment, money, fashion, religion, war, animal rights, sexuality, careers, food, art, transport, race, gender, language, sport... The list is a long one. Often it may simply be other people expressing their personal opinions, but sometimes it is a deliberate attempt to persuade our children to hold the same beliefs or attitudes. Sometimes financial gain is the motive – advertisements give children so many ideas about the 'next thing' they want. Sometimes other people are looking to justify their own actions by pressurizing their friends into doing the same things. Smoking, sex, drugs and drinking are cases in point.

Let's take a closer look now at some of the influences our children are under outside the family.

Television

Statistics tell us . . .

- The average father spends three minutes a day in 'quality' conversation with his children.
- The average mother spends five and a half minutes a day in 'quality' conversation.
- The average child spends three hours a day watching television.
- Children under five watch an average of two hours' television each day.

Some children have televisions in their bedrooms and many sitting rooms are arranged around the television, with meals often being eaten in front of it. If this is so, the chances are that many of the children's values and views will be shaped by what they see on television. Of course, television is part of our culture and much about it is good – but it is worth-while being careful about what our children watch, and when they watch it. You might like to use a video recorder to record programmes that you know your children would enjoy, so that the programme is available when you are ready to watch it, not only when the TV timetable dictates.

A letter in *The Times* newspaper (Feb 11th 1999) expressed a very important point about children's programming. It referred to some comments which had been made about *Blue Peter*, a children's programme that has stood the test of time and is watched by millions of children every week. It is very specifically a children's programme for children.

From Mrs S. Denniston

Sir, We are informed that Stuart Miles, the presenter of *Blue Peter*, is leaving the programme as it affords too 'twee' and 'comfort blanket' an approach to life (report Feb 8th later editions).

Perhaps Mr Miles has grown up. For too many children, however, childhood is increasingly short and 'hard hitting'. Is it a bad thing that a programme aimed at children should not set out to 'shock or offend'? That the programme makers at *Blue Peter* aim to inform and educate within the realm of childhood should be applauded. It is a rare thing as we force our children towards an ever younger understanding of an adult world.

Let us be brave. Let us err on the side of caution with our children.

Wise words from God's word

The Bible says, 'Whatever is true, whatever is noble, whatever is right, whatever is pure, whatever is lovely, whatever is admirable . . . think about such things' (Philippians 4:8). Does what our children watch fit into this category? Some of the children's cartoon films, for example, are frightening and sometimes unnecessarily violent. There are so many lovely things in this world. How much better for our children to focus on those things. There are many good children's films, and some very good children's programmes on television, but we have to be selective and not just assume that because it is on children's television it is helpful or healthy to watch. Christian videos are also available for hire or purchase, and they offer wonderful opportunities to fill our children's minds with good things.

Computers

It is not just the television that now consumes our children's time, but computers as well. Articles have been written about computers being used as 'virtual childminders', and it is essential to remember that not everything about computers is educational and good.

Computers are part of our world today, and of course it is a good thing to train our children in how to use them and get the most from them. In doing this, we will be equipping them for life in the working world. However, children who are left to their own devices on a computer can end up playing games which are often unnecessarily violent or sexually graphic. Likewise, the Internet can be a great resource for family life, but it also contains many adverts and websites that could rob our children of their childhood.

Here are some suggestions for keeping computers in their place.

- Use computers, but remember to give equal time to playing with your children and encouraging them to play together. It is play that fosters the development of social, language and thinking skills.
- Keep home computers in the 'public' parts of the house, not hidden away in bedrooms.
- Restrict the time any one child can spend on a computer, and vet the games and programmes used.

School

Often we have little control over who will teach our children when they are at school, and inevitably the teachers' attitudes will be passed on to our children. However, school life is so influential in the lives of our children that we believe it should be a place where we become involved if we possibly can. This might be through offering classroom help, or by becoming part of a parent committee or governing body.

We should also be aware of what material is being used in our schools. What books are they reading in class, for example? Recently our daughter was required to read a book that she said she found frightening. We encouraged her to explain this to the teacher, who excused her from reading the particular book that was upsetting her. So often it just takes a quiet word in a teacher's ear for things to change.

Schools are there to help our children to learn, and the majority of teachers are very open to help and suggestions from parents as long as we do not take over. They have a job to do and they do it in a professional and efficient way. Let's ensure that we work *with* the teachers who have care of our children, so that we can support them as well as have them support us and our children.

Friends

After their family, our children's friends will have the greatest influence on them. Some of these friends will influence them positively and some negatively. We can encourage our children to choose their friends wisely. We can choose friends for our children when they are very young, and after this we can gently educate them to be wise about their friendships.

Our sons come home singing all sorts of songs about different football teams and talking about a whole variety of games and television characters that we know they know nothing about. This is simply a result of peer pressure, and it starts when they are very young. For this reason, it is good to look for opportunities to encourage friendships with those who reinforce the values we hold. In such a context, peer pressure can be a good thing! One of our daughters developed a friendship with a classmate very early on in her school life, and it was a friendship that she and we enjoyed. We therefore encouraged her in this friendship because we felt it was helpful to her in every way. Over the past nine years, these two have become 'best' friends.

Wise words from God's word

We are told in Proverbs 13:20, 'He who walks with the wise grows wise, but a companion of fools suffers harm.' The apostle Paul says in 1 Corinthians 15:33, 'Bad company corrupts good character.'

Other adults

We have already mentioned schoolteachers, but there are other adults with whom our children will interact – friends' parents, childminders, teachers of outside activities like ballet or football, church children's group leaders, and so on. All of them will influence our children in some way or another. If we are aware of them, we can encourage those relationships with adults whose values we respect and want to pass on to our children.

We have a youth minister in our church who is responsible for the work with young people aged 7–18. Our children think he is one of the greatest. They talk about him at the tea table and will often comment on what he has said. He is someone who will have a positive effect in the lives of our own and many other people's children, so we make every effort as a family to support all that he does.

We are also proactive in looking for other adults who can be 'significant others' for our children. Historically, children would have lived in close proximity to their grandparents, aunts, uncles and cousins, who would all have had a share in raising those children. This is often not the case today, so it is good to look for other adults who can take up such a mentoring role.

We have developed a close relationship with one particular couple, Darren and Karen, who have both become significant others for our children. Because of our relationship with them, they have taken an active interest in the lives of our children, often coming to birthday teas, ballet shows, football games and so on. More than this, they are happy to spend time with the children individually. One of our sons, for example, has developed an interest in woodwork and Darren invited him round to help build a cupboard in his home. These two friends are a real blessing to us and our children, and life would not be nearly as rich without them.

Another relationship that we, and especially our children, enjoy as a family is with a single young lady called Annette, whom we have 'adopted' in a completely unofficial fashion! Annette often comes for Sunday lunch and recently came with us for a weekend away. Her friendship with the children means that they value her opinion and she has become a 'significant other' for them.

It is a great thing, too, when another adult takes an interest in the children and gets them involved in the sorts of things that we also have a passion for but may not have been so successful in getting them to do. A lady in our church, Julie, has a particular heart for refugees and asylum seekers. Recently, during National Refugee Week, she and a team of helpers put on a party for local refugee children. She felt that, as well as adult helpers, it would be good to have some children who could help host the refugee guests and give them a really great time. She asked whether our children might be willing to help. More than that, she took the trouble to telephone them and speak to each in turn, explaining what would be involved. The party was a great success and our children had a wonderful time, quite apart from any helping role they performed. Afterwards, Julie wrote to each child, thanking them for all they had done – something that clearly demonstrated to them the value of their contribution. We hope that our children will catch the vision of serving others and realize the benefits that come with such a lifestyle. We were very thankful that Julie helped our children in a small way to see those benefits.

We have mentioned four particular people here, but there are many others in our church family who affect our children's lives in a wonderful way. We want to say, too, that we believe the extended family has an important place in family life. Grandparents often have more time than we do to play with and read to the children. Uncles, aunties and cousins are all part of the picture too. We and our children gain immense pleasure from these relationships, which bring so much richness for our family.

The role of mentoring from one generation to another is a valuable thing in the lives of our children. The benefits of developing such relationships are far-reaching and our children gain much from the wisdom and input these other adults are able to offer. There are times when they have insights that we ourselves do not have, and we are grateful to them for their help in bringing up our children.

It is worth saying that we too might have an opportunity to be a 'significant other' for someone else's child. What a great thing to bless others in the way that we have been blessed ourselves.

Taking stock

There are so many influences that might affect our children. Take a few moments to look at the list below, and think about how many hours each week your children spend with this person or doing that activity. Then ask yourself how helpful or unhelpful that person or activity is.

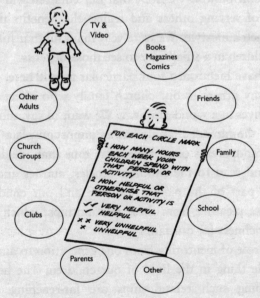

TV & Video

Books Magazines Comics

Other Adults

Friends

Church Groups

Family

Clubs

School

Parents

Other

FOR EACH CIRCLE MARK
1 HOW MANY HOURS EACH WEEK YOUR CHILDREN SPEND WITH THAT PERSON OR ACTIVITY
2 HOW HELPFUL OR OTHERWISE THAT PERSON OR ACTIVITY IS
✓✓ VERY HELPFUL
✓ HELPFUL
✗✗ VERY UNHELPFUL
✗ UNHELPFUL

Perhaps it is also worth asking the following questions.

- Who has the greatest influence on my children?
- Am I happy about this influence?
- Does anything need changing?
- Who else is helping us to bring up our children?

Our children's relationship with God

It is good to be aware of all these influences in the lives of our children, but let's not make the mistake of concluding that parenting is nothing more than providing the best possible outside influences. It is not enough to assume that if we can protect them, always be positive with them and provide them with the best possible experience, then our children will turn out OK. We cannot take it as read that good shaping influences will automatically produce good children. If we do, we are forgetting that our children themselves have an active part to play in their own development. Our children respond to their surroundings, to the influences around them, according to where their hearts are.

Children are not just passive receivers of outside influences. They are active responders.

As our children interact with their childhood experience, their response will be affected by all sorts of things, including the following:

- Whether they have *good relationships within the family*,

where opinions and problems can be raised and discussed.

- Whether they are *aware of the values of the family* and to what extent they have taken on those values (see Chapter 6 for more on this).
- Whether they have *good relationships with other trusted adults* to whom they can go to discuss things.
- Whether they have *good friendships with peers* who encourage them to fulfil their potential.
- Whether they have been taught to question and *think things through for themselves.*
- Their *perception of God.* Some children are growing in an understanding of who God is and are enjoying being in relationship with him. They are seeking to make sense of life through that relationship, and this will inevitably affect their response to their childhood experience and to our efforts to reach their hearts.

Part of our task as parents is to help our children to worship and honour God in their lives. Our children's understanding of who God is and their own relationship with him will affect their response to life. How can we encourage our children in their relationship with God?

1. Pray for them

Praying for our children does not necessarily mean that they will be accident-free and live long, healthy lives. However, if we pray regularly that our children will develop their own relationship with God, it does mean that there will always be a channel open between their lives and God.

As our children have grown, we have enjoyed seeing some

of our prayers answered. I am sure that we are not the only parents who pray as we see our children off to school for the first time, or as they share how they feel when they are alone in the playground with 'no friends'. We remember praying specifically for one of our sons who was struggling because he had no special friend of his own age at church. We were so thankful when God seemed to answer that prayer by pointing out to us someone who was already in the church but who had not yet become a friend.

We can also pray for our child's future partner. The chances are that any future husband or wife of our children will already be born. What a blessing to pray for that person now.

Why not pray also for the children yet to be born? Prayer for the unborn child, or even for the child yet to be conceived, is important. And when a baby girl is born, she has within her all the eggs that will later in life produce children, God willing. So start praying as soon as you can, for God is involved in every part of conception. Psalm 139 reminds us:

> For you created my inmost being;
> you knit me together in my mother's womb.
> I praise you because I am fearfully and wonderfully made;
> your works are wonderful,
> I know that full well.
> My frame was not hidden from you
> when I was made in the secret place.
> When I was woven together in the depths of the earth,
> your eyes saw my unformed body.
> (verses 13–16)

As a church, we hold 'prayer showers' for women as they

are about to have their babies. One of the women in the
church, usually someone with pastoral oversight of the
expectant mother, invites round on her behalf a group of
about twelve women, about two weeks before the birth
date. The father-to-be usually arranges to be out – and in
fact the men sometimes gather together for their own support evening. The prayer shower begins with some worship
and perhaps a reading from Scripture. Then there is an
opportunity for the expectant mother to share all her concerns and prayer requests in relation to the forthcoming
arrival of her baby. Everyone then gathers round to pray.
The testimonies from these evenings have been hugely
encouraging for those involved.

**The greatest prayer we can offer for our
children is that they will know a relationship
with their heavenly Father. Children as young
as three can understand enough to have a
meaningful relationship with him.**

---

2. Pray with them

Even one-year-old children can copy you in praying, and
very quickly begin to understand the concept of prayer. As
they get older and you help them to bring God into everything – anxieties, problems, joys – by encouraging them to
pray, they will quickly begin to do it for themselves.

- Pray with them before they go to sleep at night.
- Point out to them answers to prayer.
- Pray with them about world situations.

A while ago there was a national news item about two children who had gone missing on their way to school. We talked about this with our children and prayed together for the girls, who were missing for about three days. When the news broke that they had been found, we were all able to rejoice and thank God for returning them safely to their families.

- Pray about things that trouble them or have hurt them.
- Pray at the start of a long car journey.
- Pray before a meal – at home and in restaurants.

Try to make prayer the most natural thing in the world.

3. Be open with your children about your own faith

Look for ways to remind the children of God's goodness as often as possible. On arriving at a holiday cottage recently, the children of some friends of ours raced upstairs to see their bedrooms for the next week. 'It's fantastic to be here!' they said. Their mum replied, 'Yes, isn't God good to provide us with a holiday and a home to come to?' It benefits all of us to remember to be thankful to God for the good things we have.

One of the things we love doing as a family is going for walks together, especially when they are full of adventure. On one recent walk, the footpath disappeared after only a few fields. The adventure began as we looked for ways to reach our destination. With each new challenge came an opportunity to thank God for his goodness. The lambs in the field, the birds in the hedgerows, the little waterfalls – all these provide an opportunity to talk about God and his ways.

- Tell them all that you know about God so that they learn from you.
- Talk to them about ways in which God has answered your own prayers.
- Share with them how God has met a need for you or someone else.

4. Let them see you reading your Bible and praying

It is important for children to know that you are really living out what you talk to them about. Children learn so much from copying, and if they see us spending time with God they will want to do the same. We all know that we give time to what we value. If our children see us doing that, they will come to know that it is real for us, and in turn it will be real for them.

5. Encourage them to enjoy the Bible themselves

For the older children, consider buying them a Bible of their own and some fun Bible teaching notes to help them understand what they are reading. Working through the notes with them will let them know that you think it is important.

For younger children, a toddler Bible or very simple notes are good. Read them Bible stories and talk to them about how these stories apply to their own lives. There are so many good Bibles available today, and many are designed so that we can read a story a night to our children. In the early years, when children love their parents to read to them each night, try reading a regular story and then a Bible story. This means that they will be getting two stories and learning about God at the same time.

6. *Let them see you worshipping in church.*

If we make worship a priority in our lives, both in and out of church, then our children will do the same. We might talk about the songs we sing in church and explain why we sing what we do. We might also talk about why we worship God and why it is important to us.

Encourage your children to listen to children's worship tapes, and learn the songs with them so that you can sing them at other times to help them learn lessons from the Bible.

7. *Read them books with a Christian message*

Fill their minds with good things. There are so many good books around, and we can encourage our children to enjoy many of them by reading with them or buying them as little presents.

8. *Worship together as a family*

Read the Bible together and talk about it. Allow an opportunity for everyone to talk and to share what they would like prayer for, and have everyone pray for each other. Use these times as opportunities for strengthening and encouraging your children's own personal relationship with God. Family time is a great chance to do this.

In this chapter we have looked at some of the main influences on our children's lives. These come both from personal relationships (inside and outside the family) and from the activities they are involved in. Our children's relationship with God is, we believe, also fundamental. All these things will have an impact in determining how our children's hearts are shaped. In the next chapter we will develop further this idea of reaching our children's hearts, looking at the kinds of things we are seeking to place there and how we might go about it.

Taking it further

1. Review the list of influences on your children and think about any changes you may want to make.
2. Consider your child's relationship with God. Look at how you might encourage him or her to develop that relationship.

6

Transmitting Values

In Chapter 1 we thought about some of our hopes and dreams for our children. We thought about being families who do not just seek to survive, but who have vision. For many people, ourselves included, that vision would involve a desire to bring up children who are confident, capable, secure, happy, courageous, fun-loving, honest, considerate, diligent – children who will ultimately make a difference in this world. Is there anything we can do to help our children towards this? The answer to this question has to be, 'Yes, we can.'

When we decorate our house I (Mark) generally get the job of moving the furniture, and rubbing down the walls and the woodwork. This job takes hours, or at least it seems that way. Then the filling and undercoat need to be put on. Finally, I put on the gloss. The room smells of fresh paint and I feel satisfied, but it still looks a mess. Lindsay is better than I am at putting up wallpaper, so she comes along after the preparation has been done and hangs the paper. In a matter of hours, the room is finished and all that anyone can see is glossy woodwork and beautifully hung wallpaper.

Friends who visit comment on how well the paper is put up and how it brightens up the room. What a great choice of pattern! Look how well it goes with the carpet! Doesn't it match the curtains well? No mention is made of the way the walls have been rubbed down, or how beautifully flat the paper is because of the preparation that has been done. Nor does anyone mention how well the woodwork has been filled, how well the undercoat was obviously put on – and nor would you expect them to. Nonetheless, it is the preparation that helps to make the finish so good.

This chapter is all about the preparation we put into our children's lives. If we are to bring up children who are not just outwardly obedient, having learned to do the right things mechanically, but who will go on to live good lives, choosing to do what is right rather than wrong, then we will be looking to train their hearts. This is, of course, what we are all trying to do as Christians. We are seeking to train our own hearts, to live lives that honour God, so that through our lives others will see something of God in us.

**Our aim as parents is to bring up children
whose lives are an outward expression
of a right heart.**

In the last chapter we saw the importance of encouraging our children to have a relationship with God, and we noted that one of the benefits of this relationship will be that they will develop hearts that are open and responsive to all that we seek to pass on to them. In addition to nurturing them in their faith, we can also teach them or place in their hearts the values that are important to us and that we find in the Bible.

Family values

As we said in Chapter 4, every family has values – particular standards, attitudes, ideas and beliefs that affect how that family operates. The answers to questions like the ones below will offer clues about particular family values.

- What is a priority and what is not?
- What causes Mum and Dad to 'go mad', and what goes by without them even commenting?
- Are material possessions important, or do friendships and family relationships have greater value?
- Is keeping the house tidy too important to allow friends home for pizza and Coke, or are people welcome in our home at any time?
- What attitudes do the children grow up with?
- Is a relationship with God central to family life, or does life go on from week to week without reference to him?

So what are our values? What values are we passing on to our children? If we are going to place these values in our children's hearts, we need first to have identified what they are. Sometimes values are so in-built that we live them out without being conscious of them. Our values can change, too. Especially if we became Christians in adulthood, it might be that we gradually had to adopt a new set of values because those with which we grew up were not in keeping with what we found in the Bible.

One of the values with which Lindsay grew up was 'People matter'. In her home, if something got broken, as long as it was a result of an accident and not carelessness, her father would say, 'It doesn't matter. Things aren't important. It's people that matter.' Another value that was prevalent in her home was that loyalty and commitment are important. In other words, if you join a club or organization such as the Brownies or a sports team, then you should always turn up, unless you are ill, because you will be letting people down if you do not.

We know someone who grew up in a family where outward appearances were thought to be very important. In other words, it did not matter what problems there might be within the family as long as things looked fine from the outside. In adulthood and as a Christian, she has had to leave that particular family value behind and adopt healthy ones in its place.

- What values did you grow up with in your family?
- What values do you have now?

It might help to look at the list below and see whether or not you agree with the statements.

- God is number one in our lives. No person or thing is more important. We should make time to worship him and should never speak in a way that is dishonouring to him.
- Family relationships are important, especially the ones between parents and children.
- It is wrong to take another person's life.
- Marriage is a God-given thing and is the right place for sex.
- We should always pay for what we want to own unless

we are given it as a gift. Stealing is always wrong.

- Honesty and truth are crucial for the smooth running of society. Lies are wrong, as is the dishonesty of putting someone else in a bad light.
- It is wrong to be jealous of what other people have and think that you should have it as well. People are more important than possessions. Other people matter.
- We should respect the law and honour all those in authority over us. Breaking the law will generally hurt others in the end.

You may notice that this list is based on the Ten Commandments (see Exodus 20:1–17). If you find that you agree with what it contains, then the chances are that many, if not all, of your family values are based on the Bible.

Take a few moments to think through the list above and place them in order of importance for you.

It is these family values that we want actively to place in the hearts of our children. We want to give them a framework for life. We want to place in their hearts values that are good, honest and biblical. How can we do this?

The conscience

The heart is very closely linked with the work of the conscience, and in fact the Bible speaks of the conscience and the heart in the same way. It is out of our 'heart' or 'conscience', our understanding of what is right and wrong, that our attitudes and values come.

We are made in the image of God, and so in each of us there is a conscience which contains the ability to choose between right and wrong. It is as though God has made us with a basic sense of right and wrong, of good and evil. We have this innate framework, which we are then able to fill from life's experiences and learning. God made us with a conscience, but he left much of it empty. He placed there the framework – his ideas – and then left us to fill it or develop it with the values by which we choose to live our lives. We are able to adapt and shape our own value system. Moreover, while our children are young, we have the opportunity to place in their heart, in their conscience, the values we feel are important.

Wise words from God's word

Psalm 119:11 sums it up: 'I have hidden your word in my heart that I might not sin against you.' Just as David, the writer of the psalm, hid God's word in his own heart, so we can 'hide', or place, God's word in our children's hearts.

Let's look more closely at how we can shape the conscience with God's values – values which, if we so choose, can be our own family values.

The value library

The heart, or conscience, is the area which receives and stores values – it is a 'value library'. The Bible says in Deuteronomy 6:6–7, 'These commandments that I give you today are to be upon your hearts. Impress them on your children.' We, the parents, are to fill the 'shelves' in our children's hearts with good values. We place in our children's hearts the values of honesty, respect, fairness, wisdom, honour, gentleness and patience, in order that they may possess strong resources to draw from when they have moral choices to make.

It is worth mentioning at this point that just because a child knows right from wrong, it does not necessarily mean they will *choose* right every time. That is why we stressed in the last chapter the importance of encouraging our children to open their hearts to Jesus. As God grows the fruit of the Spirit in our children, such things as self-control begin to be seen, and it is these qualities that can help our children to choose right rather than wrong.

A child caught our eye the other day at a toddler session. On the table was a plate of biscuits. While it was evident that, naturally, this child was desperate to take one and pop it in her mouth, she somehow knew that she needed to wait for her mother, and managed to resist until such time as her mother arrived and saved the day. Self-control is a very attractive attribute and will benefit our children considerably if they are able to acquire it. It is also worth remembering that it can be learned at a much earlier age than you might think.

Value search system

So we place good values into the hearts of our children. We try to teach them about honesty and right relationships and so on – and we seek to model those things in our own lives as well. From this store, or 'library', of knowledge our children are able to find answers to the dilemmas that life throws at them. As adults, we are faced with new decisions every day. Whether we are out shopping, in the office or watching television, we are constantly confronted with ethical issues which require us to make the right moral choices. For each new situation we meet, a 'search system' comes into play, scanning the shelves of the value library – our conscience – for the corresponding value. If such a value is found, we can apply it to the situation. If, on the other hand, no corresponding value is found, the process ends and we take no action.

Imagine, for example, that it is a Saturday afternoon and you and the children have wandered into town. You find yourself in the children's section of the local bookshop. You need to buy a present and, as you browse, you do not notice until too late that your two-year-old has reached out of her buggy, grabbed one of the books off the shelf and torn two of the pages in it. Hurriedly you take the book from her and close it up, looking over your shoulder to check that no one has seen, pop it back on the shelf and surreptitiously make for the door.

It is only as you are leaving that your value search system comes into play. You begin to ask yourself whether you should really be walking away from the book your child has just ruined. And so begins the search up and down the 'shelves' of your conscience or value library. You come up against the value that if you damage or destroy someone else's property, the right thing to do is to replace the item or pay for it. Your conscience prompts you to act, and so you turn back, find the book, go to the sales assistant and pay for the damaged book. This is the kind of value that we need to put into our children's hearts. You may have found, as you have sought to live this way, that people are pleasantly surprised and often respond well to your honesty.

Some time ago, Lindsay took the children into the Body Shop to do some shopping. On arriving home from their trip she realized that our son, who was then aged two, had taken one of the hair slides from the shelf and brought it home without Lindsay noticing. When the slide was discovered, our eldest daughter said, 'Oh, Mummy, we must take that back. We haven't paid for it.' At the next opportunity we called in to the Body Shop to return the hair slide. The assistant clearly thought we were unusual, but admitted to thinking that what we had done was right, even though she might not have done it herself!

Honesty

To highlight the benefits of inputting these values into our children's lives, let's look more closely at the example of honesty and see how we can encourage it in a practical way in the family. Honesty is very powerful in building strong, healthy relationships within the family and for that reason is well worth working at. Without honesty, it is very difficult to maintain a bridge of trust between family members. It will not always come easily – all children and adults are capable of being dishonest – but the rewards of an honest, open relationship are worth striving for.

There will be times in every family when honesty takes a back seat, and the question is, how do we deal with it? The two most likely occurrences will be:

- Not telling the truth (or lying)
- Taking things that belong to someone else (or stealing)

How do we handle these when they occur?

Not telling the truth

Bear in mind the age of your child. A child less than three years old will not understand the impact that his untruthfulness has on his relationships. An older child will, however, so begin by trying to get him to be honest by talking with him. If that does not work, try talking generally about the importance of honesty and help him to appreciate that, in order for us to trust each other, we need to be truthful with one another.

We would suggest that most parents tend always to look for the best in their children, so would not want to resort to calling any of them liars. If, however, you are aware that your child is regularly dishonest, it is important that you try to get behind that behaviour. There are two aspects to consider:

- *The motive behind the lie*. This will help you try to correct it. Is your child wanting attention, trying to escape responsibility, or simply copying someone else?
- *Your child's general level of honesty*. Telling a lie in a moment of weakness is different from habitual lying, and should be dealt with differently.

If he really will not come clean, he may get away with it this time, but at least your relationship will remain intact. And your child will respect you for not disciplining him when you are not sure what really happened.

Taking things that belong to someone else

Again there are two aspects to consider before you take any action:

- *The seriousness of the theft*. Taking a packet of crisps from the cupboard without permission is not the same as taking £5 from Mum's purse.
- *The context*. Taking a packet of crisps from the cupboard is not the same as taking a packet of crisps from the newsagents.

Dishonesty within the family reflects on the child; dishonesty outside the family reflects on the family.

It is worth saying that stealing is not always a tangible thing. You can steal someone's time, or you can steal their reputation through gossiping about them. Gossip is something about which God feels strongly (see Proverbs 6:19). It is difficult to restore someone's reputation once it has been damaged. Wise parents will teach their children the importance of being careful about what we say concerning other people.

How do we input these family values?

In their very early years, we will be directing our children by using quite a few negatives. So we find ourselves saying 'No' or 'Don't touch' several times a day. At this stage our parenting will involve many restrictions, warnings and consequences. We do this because, before the age of about three, a child does not have the capacity to understand reason, the rightness or otherwise of his actions, or how those actions relate to those around him. A child therefore learns and is motivated by tangible consequences, such as being removed to his cot – something which acts as a trigger to remind him next time not to do the same thing again.

From around the age of three, however, it is important to change the approach from this negative form of training to a much more positive form of shaping. Now we can begin to input positively into our children's conscience. This will involve instruction, encouragement and reinforcement. We are now looking to move our children's motivation for doing the right thing from 'if I do that I'll get into trouble' to actively choosing for themselves to do the right thing. This will constantly involve us in providing the reason 'why' in answer to many of their questions and as an accompaniment to our instructions.

So how is this change of approach seen in the family? In our house, when the children wake up in the morning they stay in their beds and read quietly until Mum and Dad get up and the day begins. Our older children know the reason behind this: if they were to get up and play, the noise would wake those who were still sleeping and the morning would start badly for everyone. A few years ago one of our children, then about two and a half, moved from a cot into a bed. She was too young to understand the reason why she should stay in bed in the morning, so we simply said that she must not get out of bed until we said and that if she did, she would have to sleep in her cot again. Because she did not want to lose the privilege of sleeping in a bed, she learned to stay in it! In addition, our older daughter, who shares a room with her little sister, stayed in bed as quietly as possible in order not to make it difficult for the little one – although she was quite old enough to climb in and out of bed to get a book or turn the light on without disturbing anyone. Thus it was training through negative consequences that taught our daughter to do what the others were doing because they understood the reason why.

In time, our children should begin to do things because they are the right things to do. The value library begins to act by itself. They may even start to explain to each other why a certain course of action is right. Then you can really feel you are getting somewhere!

Encouraging a healthy conscience

It is so important to make that change from negative to more positive training. Otherwise we risk frustrating our children, who will not understand the reasons behind what we are requiring of them, even though they have the capacity to do so.

A healthy conscience is what we are looking to develop in our children. A healthy conscience is marked by the attitude, 'I ought to do this because it is right.' It is motivated by choosing to do the right thing. Obedience becomes attractive simply because it is the right thing to do.

An unhealthy conscience, on the other hand, is marked by the attitude, 'I must do this or else I'll be punished.' Here the motivation for obedience is fear of punishment. If our children grow up with an unhealthy conscience, we are preparing them to live a life in which they constantly feel guilty or fear feeling guilty should they get something wrong.

A healthy conscience can more easily develop if:

- Children know that their parents love them unconditionally, rather than believing that their love depends on good behaviour.
- Parents try to respond to bad behaviour by correcting it and moving on rather than looking to make the child feel guilty. (This will protect our children from thinking they have to behave in order to avoid feeling guilty.)
- Parents can seek to input strong values and explain the reason for upholding them.

We want to bring up our children to be confident in themselves about what is or is not the right thing to do in a given situation. We want them to act not through fear of guilt or punishment, but through a sheer desire to do the right thing.

Take a moment now to ask yourself the following questions.

- What values are you placing in your children's hearts?
- How are you placing them?
- Are you aware of living out and encouraging in your children good or biblical values, emphasizing that other people matter?

Here is a fun test to do on yourself to see what sort of conscience you have. Give yourself a score for each statement, according to the scale given below, then match your total to the scores given at the end of the test.

The Healthy Conscience Test

Scale
    1 = Never true of me
    3 = Sometimes true of me
    5 = Half yes/half no
    7 = Usually true of me
10 = Always true of me

1. I am uncomfortable in a discussion where my view or opinion is different from that of the other person.
2. I find it hard to say 'no' when someone makes a request of me which would add to an already over-busy schedule.

3. When a friend is distant or preoccupied, I tend to assume it is because of something I have done wrong.

4. I often end up doing something I do not really want to do for fear that if I do not, people will criticize me in my absence.

5. When someone says they want a meeting with me next week but do not say what it is about, I spend a lot of time worrying that I have done something wrong.

6. I often find myself offering to do things for people out of guilt rather than a genuine desire to help them.

7. I am easily unsettled if my parents-in-law do not agree with the way I discipline my child(ren).

8. I am afraid to discipline my child(ren) for fear that he/she/they will not love me any more.

9. I feel guilty when I cannot comply with what my mother or father is asking of me.

10. I pay more attention to the criticism of one person than to the praise and admiration of the other 99.

11. I constantly look for affirmation from those closest to me.

12. I often find myself quickly apologizing in order to make peace, even though I do not feel I am to blame.

Total scores

91–120	Excessively unhealthy conscience
73–90	Fairly unhealthy conscience
54–72	Moderately unhealthy conscience
41–53	Slightly unhealthy conscience
29–40	Healthy conscience
12–28	Possibly a hardened conscience!

Taking it further

1. Look for opportunities to explain the reason 'why' when children ask questions about everyday activities.
2. Try to be aware of your own responses to situations and ask yourself why you do what you do.

7

Training and Obedience

Our experience has been that most people are eager to turn to the chapter on discipline in any book on parenting. And, inevitably, this is a subject that arouses many different emotions and opinions. Our perspective, however, is that if we are putting into place the sorts of things we have been concerned with in Chapters 1–6, then the two chapters that follow become less important, because we find ourselves having to do less correcting than might otherwise have been the case. Nevertheless, it is a very important subject. It is unfortunate that the word 'discipline' has lost its proper meaning today. It has come to imply punishment or smacking. Real discipline is much more than this. Its focus is on reaching and training the heart.

Wise words from God's word

Proverbs 23:19 says, 'Listen, my son, and be wise, and keep your heart on the right path.' We read in Luke 6:45, 'The good man brings good things out of the good stored up in his heart.' And Proverbs 22:15a says, 'Folly is bound up in the heart of a child.'

Children naturally sometimes do silly and unwise things. The job of Mum and Dad is to give instruction to our children so as to encourage them to have hearts that are wise. This is the purpose of discipline, and when looked at in this broader context it becomes an area of exciting opportunity rather than one of tension and stress.

Proverbs 22:6 says, 'Train a child in the way he should go, and when he is old he will not turn from it.' And Proverbs 1:7b–9 tells us, 'Fools despise wisdom and discipline. Listen, my son, to your father's instruction and do not forsake your mother's teaching. They will be a garland to grace your head and a chain to adorn your neck.'

Although verbal instruction will be the starting point of discipline, it is not the only way a child will learn. Other ways include correction, appropriate consequences, incentives, rewards, encouragement and affirmation, which we will look at more closely in the next chapter. We would like to start our thinking about discipline, however, by considering how our children respond to us when we ask them to do something. We want to look at the question of obedience, and to see how this works out in our families.

Obedience is probably not the most fashionable concept these days, but when it is evident it is a very attractive thing, and it brings real peace and harmony to the family. We believe that our aim as parents can be obedience on the part of our children. The Bible encourages this in many different places, and it does so for the good of our children. Colossians 3:20, for example, says, 'Children, obey your parents in everything, for this pleases the Lord.' God's intention in giving us our children was that we should give them instruction and correction as well as care and nurture. That was his plan.

THIS WAY!

Have you noticed how easy it is for us to go along with the children for the sake of a bit of peace and quiet in the home? Have you realized how readily we sometimes take on the role of adviser rather than parent? Often we have little confidence that our children will do as we ask. We therefore see children making decisions and parents suggesting options. Sometimes our children have so much choice that by the time they reach the age of ten or eleven they are their own bosses and parents have very little control at all.

One summer, while we were taking our children to buy ice creams at the beach, we queued up behind a mother and her daughter who were talking about the ice cream they were about to buy. The mother explained to her daughter that she, the mother, would carry the ice cream back to where they were based on the beach and that her daughter could eat it there. The little girl kicked up a bit of a fuss about this and insisted that she should be allowed to carry the ice cream herself. The mother explained that she might fall or drop the ice cream, but still the daughter insisted. I watched this little incident with interest, wondering what the outcome would be. When they reached the front of the queue the poor mother, worn down by the little girl's pleading, handed her the ice cream. It takes a while to buy seven ice creams, and as we eventually started to walk back to where we were based, I noticed the mother and her young daughter rejoin the queue. The ice cream had been dropped in the sand. I heard the mother say that this time *she* was going to carry it back!

Let's acknowledge our responsibility. Let's see ourselves not as care providers but as parents, with a responsibility to care for, nurture, correct and instruct our children. There are many benefits for our children in this.

- To live in obedience to parents brings *safety* for our children. In Ephesians 6:1–3, God has drawn a circle of great blessing. It says, 'Children, obey your parents in the Lord, for this is right. "Honour your father and mother" – which is the first commandment with a promise – "that it may go well with you and that you may enjoy long life on the earth".' If children live within that circle of obedience to their parents, things will go well. It is a place of safety.

- It will help them in their own *relationship with God*. It will be through obedience to God that they will learn to hear his voice and respond to him.

- Children who have been taught and encouraged in obedience will respond well to *authority* in general (e.g. at work later in life) and will thus grow in wisdom and understanding (see Proverbs 15:5; 29:15). The Bible is full of references relating to authority. Hebrews 13:17a says, 'Obey your leaders and submit to their authority.' Romans 13:1 says, 'Everyone must submit himself to the governing authorities, for there is no authority

except that which God has established. The authorities
that exist have been established by God.'

If we are honest, many of us may not find coming under
authority the easiest thing in the world. We like to do our
own thing. It does not come easily to 'do as we are told'. Yet
we know that it is good to respect authority and to teach
our children to do the same.

Authority is needed for *order*. If it were not for authority,
we would risk our lives every time we went out in the car,
we would have no certainty that our savings were safe in the
hands of the bank or building society, and buying food from
the supermarket would become a health hazard.

Authority also helps us to be *considerate* and to think of
others. People like to walk their dogs in the park behind our
house. There is a notice in the park that asks people to clean
up after their dogs, and if they do that everyone else can
enjoy the park too. If we all just do our own thing, others
suffer – including ourselves in the end.

It is good not only to teach our children to obey the rules,
but also to talk to them about why we obey them. We said
in the last chapter how important it is to change our
approach (when our child reaches an appropriate age) from
negative to positive training, and this is closely connected to
that.

So how do we fare ourselves when it comes to authority?
We know that our children tend to copy us – they pick up
our attitudes. If they see us disregarding authority, they are
likely to do the same. If, on the other hand, we respect
authority, our children will probably follow us in that.
Recently we went to see a film that carried a 12 certificate.

Our attention was caught by a mother arguing with the ticket office attendant. Evidently she had tried to buy a ticket for her eleven-year-old son, but had been refused. 'Oh, how ridiculous!' she kept saying. 'He's nearly twelve. Why can't you let him in?' We wondered what impression of the law that young boy would be left with.

Before we look more closely at how this all works out in practice, let's just remember a couple of warnings:

1. Like our children, we can fall short too (and often do). We may need to say 'sorry' to our children, for example, if we find ourselves exploding at them.
2. Remember what Colossians 3:21 says: 'Fathers, do not embitter your children, or they will become discouraged.' We need to be thoughtful and try to avoid unnecessary exasperation.

Obedience in practice

There will be times when our children will ignore or oppose our reasonable instructions. What can we do? We can teach them how to respond. So often our children are willing to respond if we will only show them how.

When we ask our children to do something such as tidy their room or help to wash up, we can reasonably expect a response such as 'Yes, Mum' or 'Yes, Dad,' followed by a willingness to carry out what we have requested. This is not unreasonable! After all, most children will respond immediately to the request, 'Please would you get ready – I want to take you to McDonalds,' and so can surely respond just as quickly to the request, 'Please would you tidy your room'!

So often for all of us, however, a request such as 'Darling, I want you to go to bed now' is met with the reply, 'I'll go at the end of this programme,' or 'Why do I always have to go to bed so early?' We end up feeling frustrated because our children will not do as they are asked. If, however, we allow our children continually to get away with not doing as they are asked, we will in effect teach them to be disobedient. We will teach them that obedience is not a priority.

Now, we know that for all of us, almost without exception, obedience seems a tall order. It is likely, in fact, to be more of a problem for us than it is for our children. Interestingly, children often respond to their parents' resolve and nothing more. So often it is we, the parents, who unwittingly teach disobedience, while desiring obedience. Below are some of the ways in which parents might undermine their own efforts – and we all fall into these traps from time to time!

1. We threaten and repeat ourselves

When we ask our children to do something, do we really expect them to do it? How often do we find ourselves saying something like the following? 'Tommy, put your shoes on . . . Tommy, did you hear me? I asked you to put your shoes on . . . Tommy, if you don't put your shoes on, I'm going to get cross . . . Tommy, do you want me to get very cross? . . . Tommy, if you're a good boy and put your shoes on, you can have some chocolate . . . Right, no chocolate for you! . . . Tommy, if you don't put your shoes on, I'll smack you! . . . Tommy, put your shoes on! . . . Right, you've had enough warnings, I'm going to smack you . . .' At this point Tommy quickly puts his shoes on and we say, 'Good boy, Tommy.'

Our children know if we really mean what we say. They are born gamblers. They will tiptoe across the line, enjoy being naughty, and then dash back in the hope of not disturbing the sleeping giant, the parent. Obedience becomes subjective. Consequences are no longer tied to disobedience, but to the mood and whim of Mum or Dad at any particular moment.

2. We use bribes

We could all benefit from asking ourselves whether we sometimes barter with our children in order to gain their obedience. Having asked them to clear up their toys with little response, do we then say, 'Listen, if you clear up your room, then you can have an ice cream'? This will probably get the desired response in the short term, but if it continues, our children will grow up expecting rewards in return for obedience. 'What's in it for me?' will be their only motivation for obeying. Of course, children should sometimes be rewarded for their obedience, but they should not be taught to be obedient just to get a reward.

3. We negotiate in the midst of conflict

How often do our children try to negotiate with us in the midst of a conflict situation? Perhaps the babysitter has just arrived, and as you leave you say to your child, 'Up to bed at 8.30. No later.' Your child replies with, 'Oh, can't it be 9 o'clock, just this once?' And the battle begins! You try to insist on 8.30 because it is school tomorrow and it has been a busy week, but eventually your child wears you down and through sheer embarrassment in the front of the babysitter you agree to move to 8.45. What has happened? Your child has pushed you into moving the boundary and, because he has succeeded this time, he will be even more determined to do the same again next time.

4. We misuse compassion

How often do our children only see and experience our compassion and never our judgement and justice? How will they ever learn to do as they are asked if their disobedience always ends in hugs? We are not being unloving by insisting that requests from Mum and Dad are obeyed.

5. We offer too much choice

Do you have days like this one? You get up in the morning and get out your child's blue jumper and trousers and start to dress him. 'Oh, I wanted to wear my red jumper!' he says. 'OK,' you reply. You go down for breakfast and you put his Weetabix in the bowl. 'Oh, I want Cornflakes,' he says. 'OK,' you reply, as it is no trouble to change it. You get to mid-morning and you give your child a drink. 'Oh, I wanted it in my Thomas cup!' he says. 'OK, here you are.' You get to the supermarket and go to put your child in the trolley. 'I want to walk!' he shouts. 'OK then, I suppose we're not in a hurry.' You go for a walk in the afternoon, and before you can catch your breath your child runs off without waiting for you. As he runs towards a cyclist you shout, 'Come here!' – only to see the cyclist almost falling off his bike and your child calling, 'But I want to go by myself!' Fortunately no cars are coming, but you feel dreadful and wish like anything that your child would do as you say.

If we allow our children constantly to make their own choices, it is difficult for them to give up that choice when the crunch comes. How do we know when our children are ready to have choices? They are ready to have choices when they can live happily without them!

Ten tips for addressing our children

What can we do to help our children towards obedience? This is not as difficult as many would think, but it does require a willingness to be consistent and strong. Here are some basic principles of communication.

1. *Say what you mean and mean what you say*. Do not ask your child to do something unless you intend it to be carried out. If you give instructions you do not intend to see carried out, you will risk teaching your child to be disobedient.
2. *Be careful how you phrase your instruction*. Instructions phrased in the form of a question – 'Would you like to go to bed now?' – are likely to get the answer 'No!' Be firm in the way you give your instructions – 'It's time for bed now. Up you go.'
3. *Get eye contact and a verbal response*. 'Sam, look at Mum. I want you to go and put your shoes and coat on and wait by the front door.' 'Yes, Mum.' Eye contact helps the child to focus on the instruction and then to process it. A verbal response again helps with processing the instruction. When the mouth is speaking, the brain is engaged. Sometimes our children will say that they did not hear us, so it is often good to call a child's name first rather than give a straight instruction: 'Sam!' 'Yes, Dad?' 'It's bedtime, son.'

4. *Do not be too quick to repeat yourself.* Once your children know that you expect to have to say something only once, they will quickly learn that you will not say it again (unless, of course, they genuinely have not heard you). It is amazing how, once you have resolved not to repeat yourself, the children learn to respond much more quickly.

5. *Expect a response.* When you speak to your child in a way that requires an answer or action, expect a response. Often we expect no response and therefore that is exactly what we get!

6. *Provide a warning.* An instruction that interrupts or ends an activity could be preceded by a warning. This is fair and prevents us from frustrating our children. Sometimes it is appropriate to give a five-minute warning. So if you notice that it is approaching bedtime and your children are playing a game, give them a warning that they will have to finish in the next five minutes. This will help your children to prepare for the instruction, 'Off to bed now.' Obedience will be more attractive if our children know that we are aware of what they are doing and are on their side.

7. *Offer a door of escape.* You may have given a clear instruction to clear up a bedroom, but as fast as it is cleared up a little brother or sister messes it up again. The door of escape is to bring the problem to you so that you can help sort it out.

8. *Consider the setting.* Ask the question, 'Is what my child is doing in response to my instruction disobedient in this particular setting?' Imagine, for example, that you have asked your child to go up and tidy his room, and then

you go up ten minutes later to find him in his sister's room. Initially you might wonder why his room is still untidy, but if he explains that his sister has lost a book she needs for her homework and he is helping her find it, then that would alter things. It is right that he should help his sister.

9. *Be consistent*. Teaching obedience requires consistency and the giving of clear instructions. Without clear and consistent instructions, our children will be at a loss to know what to do.

10. *Remember your example*. Whatever is right for the children must also be seen as right for us. In our house, for example, we take off our shoes at the front door. The children are very quick to notice if Mum and Dad do not take off their shoes!

Remember – we can expect conflict. All children will constantly come up against situations where their own desires are in conflict with our instructions. Obedience is a lesson that we all have to learn and, as we know from our own lives, that learning curve continues throughout life. The more willing we are to be consistent in our teaching of obedience in our own families, the quicker our children will learn obedience and ultimately everyone will benefit. Inconsistency may well bring frustration for your children.

If conflict is inevitable in every family, it is helpful to view conflict not as a negative thing, but as an opportunity to move our children forward in the right direction.

• For our *younger children* (up to four years old), conflict can give us the opportunity – if we deal with it in a positive way – to establish in their minds that they need to learn to obey Mum and Dad.

- For our *older children*, we can use rebellious or inappropriate behaviour as an opportunity to help them understand that what they are doing is an indication of what is going on in their hearts, and that what will help is a change of heart.

A good safety valve

Our children have thoughts and ideas of their own which need to be heard. Once they have grasped the need for obedience (probably around the age of five), it is a good idea to teach our children that it is fine to ask us to think again about what we have asked them to do, as long as it is done respectfully. This is a good thing because:

- We may have spoken in a hurry without thinking about what we were saying. It allows us to change our mind about something which in retrospect is inappropriate.
- It protects our children from feeling that they are always in a no-win situation. It is a good safety valve for them to know that Mum and Dad will listen to them and reconsider an instruction if necessary and appropriate.

You might, for example, have asked your child to come and lay the table for tea, without realizing that he was almost at the end of a game. To come straight away would be very frustrating for him, yet not to come would amount to disobedience. At times like this, it is beneficial for everyone if our children can know that they have a say about what they have been asked to do.

You could encourage your children to respond like this:

1. On hearing us call, they begin to act straight away.
2. They ask us to rethink respectfully, and not in a whine.
3. They accept graciously that Mum and Dad have the final word.

To take the above example to its conclusion, then, your child might simply come to you and say, 'Mum, we've almost finished a game. Would you mind if we finish it before I lay the table?' And in nine cases out of ten, that would be fine.

It would be even better if we as parents could think ahead, weigh up what we are about to instruct, and check for ourselves whether it is necessary and appropriate. Perhaps your child is reading in bed and it is time for lights out. You could say, 'It's time for lights out now' – but how much better to say, 'How many more pages to the end of that chapter? Just a page and a half? OK, finish the chapter and then turn out your light.' This is so much kinder and more thoughtful, and it shows our children a better example of how to treat others.

Setting boundaries for very young children

The earlier we start this obedience training the better – in fact, we should start it as soon as a child begins deliberately to disregard our instructions. At nine months, your child may crawl to you when called. A few months later, that may change as he starts to push the boundaries. If you persist, however, and try to be consistent about bringing negative consequences, the chances are that he will come through it and learn once again to come when you call. Similarly, even before our children can talk, we can require a response, even if it is just a nod and a grunt! We can say it ourselves – 'Yes, Mummy' – and very quickly they will copy. As young as two, babies will often say 'Yes, Mummy' following a request.

Set limits and boundaries right from the start. Do not give your baby freedoms which you may later regret.

In our car we used to have two children's car seats. One was for our three-year-old and one for our 18-month-old. One day, when the three-year-old was not with us and Lindsay was in a hurry, she decided to put the younger one into her older brother's seat as it was nearest to her at the time. That was fine, until the next time we went out in the car and we went to put the younger one into her own seat. Little had we realized that for her to go into her older brother's seat had been a real privilege, and one which she did not now want to give up! She created quite a fuss for the next two or three times we went out in the car.

The purpose of setting boundaries for our children is not to take away their freedom to explore, but to give them freedom within manageable limits, according to how much they can understand. A child who is given more freedom than he can handle, or a longer rein than he can cope with, may well get himself into trouble. It is difficult for a child to enjoy freedom unless he is given that freedom within manageable limits. Below are a few ideas and tips about setting boundaries for your young child.

1. Use a playpen

If you start from when your baby is very young (say four weeks), but old enough to lie under a baby gym, he will get used to it right from the beginning. He will be able to focus more easily on his toys without the distraction of lots of space around him, and will most likely feel safe within his physical boundaries. Also, if you build playpen times into your baby's routine, you will find yourself with periods in the day when you can get on with chores in the knowledge that your baby is safe and happy in the playpen.

2. Do not be afraid to say 'no' to your baby.

'No' simply defines the necessary boundaries. The key to setting limits for your little one is not in controlling his environment by removing everything, but by training him to your voice. If your child touches something that is out of bounds, tell him 'no' firmly and offer him something else to play with. If he is at the table or in his buggy, give him a positive alternative by asking him to put his hands in his lap. If he persists, you could repeat the 'no' with a squeeze on the wrist. If he still persists, you may need to remove him from the tempting object or put him in his cot for a while.

We have noticed that if we say 'no' to a toddler and stand there waiting for him to stop doing whatever he is doing, he will very likely persist with it, trying to lure us into a battle of wills. If we say 'no, don't touch' and then walk away, he will almost always stop. It is as though our presence extends the conflict, whereas if we move away, our child can then surrender without losing face.

Similarly, if your baby is in his high chair and is disturbing the meal by shouting or playing with his food, tell him 'no' firmly and distract him by talking about something else. If he persists, you could repeat the 'no', and perhaps take his food away. If he still persists, you could either put him out of the room (still in his high chair) for a while, or simply turn his chair round to face away from the family until he is quiet.

3. Learn how to deal with tantrums

Sometimes our young children, on hearing the word 'no', will throw a tantrum. It is unlikely that a child will get through the early years without having a few tantrums, but we can teach him that there are appropriate ways of expressing emotion and that kicking and screaming is not one of them! If we can teach our child self-control at this stage, we will help him in the long run.

The way in which we, as parents, deal with tantrums will have a bearing on whether they become frequent. If the tantrum is successful – in other words, if it enables the child to get what he wants – the behaviour may reoccur. If, on the other hand, it does not achieve the desired result the first time, it is less likely to be repeated.

What can we do when a tantrum occurs? If it is a tantrum born out of frustration, because the child cannot physically manage to make the Lego model he has in his mind's eye, then we can be sympathetic and help out if required. However, if it is clearly a temper tantrum, it is good to remove the child to a cot or, if you are in public, to strap him into a buggy away from people until he has calmed down. For a child of more than about two and a half, it is good for him to know that once he has calmed down there will be a consequence to his tantrum. This will help him not to repeat it in the future.

Obedience plays a very important part in the parent/ child relationship. We would do well to remember that we are looking always to reach our children's hearts. Our aim is not to focus on behaviour, but rather to see that behaviour as an indication of what is going on in our children's hearts.

A willingness to be obedient demonstrates a heart that wants to do the right thing. That, ultimately, is what we want for ourselves and for our children.

Taking it further

1. Spend some time working on obedience, putting into practice some of the suggestions from this chapter.
2. If you have younger children, try making a game out of

your child coming the first time he is called with a 'Yes, Mum' or a 'Yes, Dad.'

3. Try giving a five-minute warning before issuing instructions and see how it makes a difference to your child's response.

8

Taking Corrective Action

In the last chapter we focused on obedience and looked especially at the benefits for our children and ourselves when obedience is part of the atmosphere in a home. Now we move on to look at the different areas into which discipline can be broken down. Discipline is much more than just punishment or smacking. Our focus here is not so much on correction, but rather on our children's hearts. A number of different approaches can be adopted which will be positive and encouraging as well as corrective.

Our children will need the positive and encouraging as well as the corrective if we are to reach their hearts and not frustrate them.

It is worth reminding ourselves of the importance of parenting with a long-term aim in mind. We are not just disciplining for the moment, nor are we just responding to a situation in order to resolve a crisis. Instead we are looking to be consistent in what we do, in order to reach our children's hearts. Here are some questions to consider.

155

- Where are our children's hearts?
- What is their motive for doing what they are doing?
- Have we given them proper instruction?
- Do they know what they are meant to be doing and why?

As we have said before, we can all train our children to behave like machines by punishing them when they misbehave. This is not our aim. Our aim is to use discipline as a whole, in order to reach the point where our children know what is right and desire to do it because it is the right thing. The various components of discipline we cover in this chapter will, we hope, help us to achieve that aim. Remember, however, that the whole thing is a process and we will not always get it right. The important thing is to think ahead and have a plan. We must not seek merely to survive the day's events!

Let's start our exploration of the different areas of discipline by distinguishing between abilities and behaviour.

Abilities

We all know as adults that in order to lead a fulfilled and healthy life certain areas require discipline. Eating a balanced diet, taking exercise, following a regular sleep pattern and making time for proper rest and relaxation are often things we have to work at: they do not necessarily come naturally to us. In the same way, there are some positive disciplines, or abilities, that our children will acquire. Abilities are not behavioural issues and so do not have a corrective side to them. They are achievements – such as riding a bike or learning to swim – that need discipline if the skills are to be acquired successfully. We can encourage our child to learn an ability chiefly through offering encouragement and praise.

Praise

Children love to be praised for their achievements, and the satisfaction of receiving that praise is a great motivator for learning something new. This sort of confirmation encourages their hearts. Praise is essential in encouraging our children to learn a discipline.

One summer, one of our boys announced that he would like to take the stabilizers off his bike once school had broken up for the holidays and he could spend time learning to ride the bike properly. Mark suggested that he might take them off there and then. I (Lindsay) was out for the day and Mark encouraged him by saying, 'What do you think Mum would say if she came home and found you could ride your bike?' He responded because he loves to receive praise, and this idea was a great incentive for him to take the stabilizers off right away. Two hours later he received that praise from Mum for the way he had learned to ride his bike.

Incentives

Another way to encourage this type of discipline is to give children an incentive to help them work at learning a particular ability. For example, you might promise them a reward for learning to ride a bike, learning to swim, giving up nappies, using a knife and fork, and so on. They will be very satisfied when they achieve their target.

Such incentives or rewards are best used for learning how to do something new, rather than as a kind of 'bribe' for sitting quietly in the supermarket trolley, which is more to do with behaviour.

Behaviour

This is an indication of what is going on inside our child's heart. It is motivated by encouragement *and* correction.

Encouragement and correction are both needed if discipline is to be truly effective.

Encouragement

There is so much we can do to encourage our children in their behaviour. We can encourage them to behave well. With forethought we can encourage them by giving them prior preparation so that they have every opportunity to do the right thing. So often children want to do the right thing, but often miss out because they have not been encouraged to do so.

As we travel to spend the day with friends, for example, we might ask the children, 'What are the "Golden Rules" when we're at a friend's house?' They will have great fun seeing how many things they can think of:

- Say 'hello' when we arrive.
- Take shoes off at the door.
- Say 'please' and 'thank you'.
- Do not charge around the house.
- Ask before playing with toys.
- Look at adults when you speak to them.

As well as reminding them of the 'Golden Rules', such an exercise also helps them to own what they have said – and this encourages them to carry out what they have spoken about. Then we can have the joy of praising them for remembering all the 'Golden Rules', and afterwards we can praise them again for doing so well while we were at our friend's house.

Correction

Sometimes, as we parents know only too well, encouragement is not always enough, and our children get it wrong and find themselves in trouble. Then comes the need for correction. Let's spend some time looking at this difficult subject in more detail.

Loving parents seek to discipline their children wisely and thoughtfully.

Wise words from God's word

'No discipline seems pleasant at the time, but painful. Later on, however, it produces a harvest of righteousness and peace for those who have been trained by it' (Hebrews 12:11). Correction is clearly an integral part of discipline. There will be times when it hurts us very much to correct our children, and we may be tempted to let things pass. In the long run, however, our children will miss out if we try to avoid correction just to make life easier for ourselves.

Before we go on to talk about correction, let's remember

another important verse from the Bible. 'Let your gentleness be evident to all' (Philippians 4:5). If we can approach correction with this in mind, we cannot go far wrong.

It is good to consider the *motivation* behind a child's particular action or behaviour before we consider taking any corrective action ourselves. Was it accidental or intentional? Was it done out of:

1. childish innocence?
2. childish thoughtlessness?
3. deliberate naughtiness?

The way in which we answer this question will determine the form of correction we use.

1. Childish innocence

When our children behave badly, it is not always deliberate. Sometimes it is simply a result of childish innocence. It may be that they do not realize, because they have never been told, that what they have done is wrong. In this case, it would be unreasonable for us to expect them to get it right.

A couple of years ago, we laid some gravel down between our patio and the garden wall. We were very pleased with the effect, because it neatened up a rather scruffy area of the garden. We were not so pleased when we went out into the garden later to find the children digging in the gravel and moving it to various other parts of the garden, including the lawn. It was very frustrating for us, but as far as the children were concerned it was just a great game. We had not told them *not* to play with the gravel, and in childish innocence they were simply occupying themselves with a new and interesting game while they played outside.

2. Childish thoughtlessness

In the summer our children love to set up camp in the garden. One day we found them dragging all their duvets and pillows (with clean covers on) out to the garden, where they put them directly on the damp and rather muddy grass. Fortunately, we found them in time and were able to send them straight back inside. It spoilt their game, but at least it saved Lindsay from having to wash all the covers again! What they were doing was not rebellious. It was childish thoughtlessness.

We will need great sensitivity and wisdom as we seek to correct our children's childish behaviour. Sometimes we will simply need to point out what has happened and give them proper instruction so that it does not happen again. At other times, when thoughtlessness is clearly the problem, a light telling-off may be required and maybe a consequence to help them remember.

3. Deliberate naughtiness

At times, as we know, children are deliberately naughty.

- They might kick a football inside the house where windows can get broken.
- They might answer back.
- They might refuse to be corrected, or refuse to comply with what we have asked them to do.

- They might be indirectly defiant by pretending not to hear, pleading ignorance, sulking or whining.

We all know our own children, and it is good to respond to deliberate naughtiness according to their general character and age. We can ask ourselves these questions:

- Have the circumstances not helped Johnny to be obedient? (If you have been waiting in the doctor's surgery for an hour and a half, for example, obedience can begin to be less attractive for any child!)
- Is he particularly tired, or hungry?
- Is he acting out of character, or is this something that often occurs and really needs to be dealt with?
- Is he unwell, or is he sickening for something?

One day I discovered our smallest children sliding on their knees on the polished hall at the back of our church. My reaction was to march in and talk to them long and hard about the possibility of knocking into people, as well as making holes in the knees of their trousers. Thinking about it afterwards, however, I realized that I had over-reacted. It struck me how difficult it sometimes is for the children when Mum and Dad spend a very long time talking after the service, and the young ones are tired and could really do with having their lunch. It is helpful to take such considerations into account before you launch into a major telling-off! Also, let's be careful when giving correction that we do not overdo it. Correction that is heavier than the crime is very disheartening for our children. We will never get it absolutely right, but we can do our best to be fair.

It is quite helpful to break things down as we consider the suitability or otherwise of a particular form of correction. Generally, deliberate naughtiness will fall into the following types – although this is only a guide and things are rarely so black and white.

a) Small incidents that need a telling-off

We are not perfect, nor should we expect our children to be. In fact, we are in danger of exasperating them if we pursue perfection. Sometimes our children will do something which they should know is naughty, or which they were corrected for three months ago, but perhaps they have genuinely forgotten or had a momentary lapse. They may know that they have to put their bikes away in the garden shed at the end of the day, for example, but have omitted to do it on this occasion. For something like this we would just give a warning and some encouragement not to forget next time.

b) Naughtiness that needs more than just a verbal telling-off

Correction might be needed for behaviour that occurs frequently, for warnings that have not been heeded, or for past habits that seem to be growing more regular again. In these cases a stronger telling-off might be appropriate, accompanied by an enforced temporary break from whatever activity the children are involved in, in order to give them some thinking time to consider what they were doing wrong and hopefully to have a 'change of heart'. Sometimes a permanent break from the activity for that day might help them to remember not to repeat whatever they were doing wrong.

Imagine that your children were given a tent one Christmas, one which needed to be treated carefully otherwise the canvas might rip or the poles break. Having explained this to the children, if you then found them and their friends all in the tent at once with the side bulging, you might remind them that if they are too rough the tent will get broken. If they continue to be overexcited in their use of the tent, you may well impose a five-minute break, hoping for a rethink and a change of heart. If they continue to mistreat the tent, the result would probably be a very firm telling-off and the removal of the tent, probably for a set period – long enough for them to miss it and think again about how they treat the tent when they play in it, so that they can enjoy it for years to come.

In terms of undesirable habits, *whining* is something that will quickly become a habit if it is left to develop. Often we tend to switch off from it to protect ourselves. If we do that, however, our children will probably persist with their whining, because eventually we tend to become worn down by it and give in. How often do we hear comments such as, 'Oh, I don't like these green bits in my lasagne!' or, 'Oh, I hate having to tidy my room!' and think it is just part of life that we have to put up with? How can we cope with whining? Can we stop it in a positive way?

- As a first step, point out that this whining is becoming a habit and that it is not an acceptable means of communicating. This in itself may have a good impact. Often we get into habits without being aware of it, and children are just the same.

- For a toddler it is often helpful just to say, 'No whining,' and have them answer you, 'Yes, Mum/Dad. No whining.' It is amazing how effective this can be, simply because, having spoken those words, they have owned the fact that whining is not acceptable.

- For a slightly older child, if requests come in a whine, you might suggest that your child goes away and has a rethink, then comes back and asks properly.
- If whining still persists, a stronger form of correction may be needed.

c) Behaviour that will need stronger action

Some things, however, will not be corrected with a telling-off or a chance to think things through. Some incidents require stronger correction. If our child has been deliberately disobedient, therefore, we will need wisdom in order to discern the gravity of the situation and to make the right decision about how to deal with it. There are various options for stronger forms of correction.

Time apart from others can work very well. Children are very social and love being with other children and adults. To be separated from other people in a cot or bedroom, or even to sit on the stairs away from the centre of activity, removes that privilege and for many is a very effective means of correction.

Smacking is another option, but one fraught with difficulty. It is often approached so aggressively that it is tantamount to physical abuse. We are all aware that the smacking of children by parents has been challenged recently through the courts, and the government has backed parents to use 'reasonable chastisement' (except in Scotland, where it has been outlawed) when disciplining their own children. It is understandable that the practice of smacking has been questioned, but we should also remember that when a parent rants and raves uncontrollably at their child it is just as violent and abusive as an out-of-control slap. The problem with out-of-control smacking is that the emotional pain caused by arbitrary, thoughtless 'discipline' is made worse by the physical abuse. The Bible does talk about 'the rod of discipline' (Proverbs 22:15; 29:15), but the interpretation of these verses is not clear cut and care is required.

Any punishment given to a child in an unthought-out, careless or vengeful fashion is abusive.

It is also important to say that smacking is not an alternative to reaching our children's hearts by teaching them to show love and self-control and to do the right thing. In fact, unless we are actively working at building loving relationships and a strong, secure home, as well as encouraging and teaching good values to our children, smacking (and any other unthought-out punishment) is really not an option. Smacking alone will not result in a changed heart.

Individual parents will need to make up their own minds about whether it is right to smack their child. If we do decide it is an option, what is important is *how* the smack is given. As parents we are all different, with different temperaments and boiling points, and different responses to the heat of the moment. For this reason we felt it would be helpful to offer a few guidelines to protect parents from reaching that out-of-control stage:

- Smacking should be reserved for wilful defiance.
- Smacking should be administered with consistency, and

not just on the days when we are short of patience. Children are born gamblers: if they are expecting a smack and do not get one, they will try it again.

- Smacking should be done in private to maintain the child's dignity, and only ever by the parent.
- Smacking should only sting, never cause physical injury.
- Most importantly, smacking should be done in a loving atmosphere, not in anger by an out-of-control parent, and the child should understand fully why he is having the smack. The child needs to be reassured of the parent's love before *and* after, and once things have calmed down he needs to know that is the end of it.

The withdrawal of a privilege is another corrective option. This might include removal of pocket money or treats, not being allowed to stay up late at the weekend, not being allowed to use a favourite toy for a set period, not being allowed to watch a favourite TV programme, and so on. We will all know what is appropriate for our own child.

Setting up logical consequences is an idea that ties in closely with withdrawal of a privilege, but the consequence would be something directly related to the behaviour in question. As our children get older, they will often respond more readily to logical consequences. If a child does not come willingly and cheerfully when you pick her up from having tea with a friend, for example, then the logical consequence might be that she does not go the next time she is invited. Alternatively, if your child is never ready on time and drags his heels when it is time for school, but is quite able to get himself ready for Cubs, which he enjoys, then you might apply a logical consequence. You might say, 'If you can't get ready for school on time, then you will have to miss Cubs this week.'

These options for responding to disobedience are not in any particular order, and sometimes more than one approach will be needed. We will need much wisdom as we decide which form of correction to use. Do not be afraid to take time to think and pray before you act. The right course of action is not always clear cut. It is important, however, to stress the need for some correction, whatever form that might take. If we seek to avoid it entirely, we will probably become very frustrated with our disobedient children. Training our children, as we said above, will involve both encouragement *and* correction.

The most important thing to remember in all of this is that our children need to know that we love them unconditionally – that whatever they do, we will always love them. If our children believe we love them, they will respond so much more readily to our discipline, be it encouragement or correction. Rob Parsons says, 'The key to a child's heart is to let her know that we love her anyway. There is no more powerful force on the face of the earth for building strong relationships than unconditional love.'[1]

Putting things right

When things have gone wrong, they need to be put right. It is a good thing for our children to learn the importance not just of receiving correction for their disobedience, but also of feeling repentant, of having a change of heart or attitude which will result in an outward change of behaviour.

Feeling repentant

It is very easy to feel regret without feeling repentant. The child who is told not to play ball by the neighbour's fence, does so and then loses the ball as it goes over may feel regret at the loss of the ball – but may not necessarily feel repentant at having played football near the fence.

To be truly repentant has an important effect in the restoration of a relationship. Just as in the Christian life we continually repent of the things which spoil our relationship with God, so it is with our relationships within the family. We can teach our children how their disobedient and selfish acts can spoil their family relationships. As we seek to reach our children's hearts with God's ideals, we will be hoping to find evidence of genuine repentance. Children of four years and up should be able to see how their actions have spoilt relationships. They should also be able to understand how, through feeling genuinely sorry, those same relationships can be put right. As family members come to see the connection between their actions and their effect on relationships, family unity is strengthened.

Forgiving and forgetting

Once genuine repentance has been felt, there is something more we can do to put things right. In the Christian life we know that Jesus offers forgiveness, through what he did on the cross, to anyone who calls out to him – but in order for that forgiveness to make right our relationship with God, we need to have repented and accepted forgiveness. It is the same in the family. We can teach our children that we are always ready to forgive them, but their part is to *ask* for that forgiveness.

**To say 'sorry' only goes part of the way:
it acknowledges a mistake.
To ask for forgiveness demonstrates
a change of heart.**

You might help your children to appreciate this powerful distinction by encouraging them to say, 'I'm sorry – will you forgive me?' when they have been disobedient or when they have fallen out with a brother or sister. Then watch how effectively and quickly it brings harmony, probably because both 'sides' have a part to play in the process and there has to be active agreement for it to take place.

Mum and Dad can say 'sorry' too

Remember how important our own example is. Forgiveness works both ways, and if we are in the wrong it will be very powerful for our children to hear us say 'sorry'.

Making amends

There is one final point to make about putting right relationships. In the Bible there is a story about a tax collector called Zacchaeus who met Jesus and became a changed man. His response was this: 'If I have cheated anybody out of anything, I will pay back four times the amount' (Luke 19:8). Sometimes we are faced with a question of personal responsibility. Saying 'I'm sorry' and asking for forgiveness is not enough if you have created a financial liability, whether accidentally or intentionally. It may be necessary to make amends in a tangible way if something tangible has been damaged.

Supposing you borrowed a travel cot from friends for your baby to sleep in while you were on holiday. And supposing your baby, having woken early one morning, managed to pull out a piece of thread and make a large hole in the side of the cot. In addition to feeling repentant and asking for forgiveness, there would be a need to put right the material damage, probably by replacing the cot.

Discipline as a positive framework

In this chapter we have seen that, if our family relationships are to be meaningful, repentance, forgiveness and making amends are all essential components of parental discipline. Inevitably in family life there will always be incidents which bring disharmony, but as we seek to teach our children the importance of putting right these relationships, our families will become stronger and our children more secure as a result. Steve Chalke says:

> Discipline should be the framework and encouragement that a loving parent creates for their child in order to help them gradually learn how to control their behaviour, and develop self-discipline. Discipline should be an enabler: a creative force designed to build maturity and consistency, helping children fit into society without being swamped by it. Discipline should give your children the self-control they need to manage what they do, both now and in the future.[2]

We hope that through the last two chapters we have communicated the message that discipline is far more than punishment. As we consistently seek to put effort into discipline as a whole, we will find that the need for correction decreases. As we put effort into shaping our children's hearts, we will find ourselves having to concentrate far less on reshaping our children's outward behaviour.

Taking it further

1. Spend some time thinking and talking about how you feel about the way you discipline your children, and discuss any changes that you want to make.
2. Find an opportunity to encourage your children in learning an ability.
3. Start putting into practice the encouragement that will help your children know how to respond on different occasions. Try, for example, giving them instruction on what is expected of them at the supermarket or at a friend's house.
4. Look out for examples of 'childish innocence' and 'deliberate naughtiness'. Is it easy to spot the difference?

9

Modelling Love and Respect

As we draw near to the final chapter, we want to focus on one of the most important things we have been trying to put across throughout the book. In an earlier chapter we referred to one of the family values that Lindsay grew up with – 'People matter'. This is, in fact, one of the central themes of the Bible. It is summed up in the commandment that Jesus gave, 'Love your neighbour as yourself' (Mark 12:31), and also in Philippians 2:3, where Paul says that we should be considerate and think of others' needs as much as our own. Lindsay's parents were seeking to teach her to care for other people, to value them and to be other-centred rather than self-centred.

We live in a materialistic age where wealth and material possessions are given great value. Many people set out to achieve solely for themselves, regardless of how that might affect anyone else. A while back we watched a programme about road rage and were astounded to hear the comments of people who believed that they were quite entitled to get out and whack someone in the face if their conduct on the road did not come up to expectations. Thankfully, those people are still very much the minority, but in today's society it is a great challenge to take seriously Jesus' teaching to love our neighbour as ourselves.

Thinking of the needs of others is a key to satisfying and harmonious relationships in all walks of life. If our children learn this when they are small, it will not only help them to have a more fulfilled life as adults, but it will also help them in their relationships with their family and friends while they are still young.

Teaching our children to value and respect other people

You might think that the ways in which we can value and respect one another are obvious, and that we all know how to do it, but actually *doing* it is sometimes the problem because it does not always come naturally. Interestingly, for children, doing it is not so much of a problem. Often they find doing the right thing much easier than adults do. Where they often fall down is in not knowing what to do in the first place.

A friend told us that one day she took her nine-year-old daughter on the bus and was surprised when she did not stand up to offer her seat to an elderly person who got on at the next stop. 'I signalled to her to get up, but she didn't respond at all!' she told us. After they got off the bus, our friend questioned her daughter about why she had been so rude. 'I didn't know you had to get up and offer your seat to an older person,' her daughter replied. At that point our friend realized that *she* was responsible for this error. She had never explained to her daughter that this was the right thing to do and why.

'People matter' is a great family value to hold, but it is meaningless unless our children know and understand how it is worked out in practice. Such a value automatically involves the way we relate to others, and we need to teach our children how they can demonstrate that they value and respect those with whom they are in relationship, so that those people know that they are valued and respected. It is a bit like the love languages we explored in Chapter 2: it is no good just knowing that you love someone; for love to be real it has to be expressed tangibly and felt by the other person.

In this chapter, therefore, we will look at the different people with whom our children find themselves in relationship. As we do that, we will think about how we can help them to grow in the attributes of love and respect, and demonstrate in their everyday lives that others are precious to them.

1. Our children's relationship with God

By its very nature, the relationship with God is very different from the others we shall cover, but it will become, we hope, the most important relationship our children will have. When they are young, we – Mum and Dad – are the ones who have the chance to teach our children and show them by our example how to love God. That is quite a privilege, but it is also a responsibility. Learning such things properly will prepare our children for a lifetime of inner peace and satisfaction. In order to love God, our children will need to learn, in childlike ways, to do the things that we do as adults.

- It will mean *becoming familiar with the Bible*, knowing and loving the stories in it, and learning about all that God has done for his people in the past.
- It will mean *learning to pray*, and remembering that when we pray the person with whom we are talking is the most important person in the whole world.
- It will mean *taking them to church*, and helping them know that the church is there as much for them as for the grown-ups. It is at church that they will see people worshipping and gradually experience doing it for themselves. If you are blessed in having lively children's worship at your church, this will happen easily. If not, you may need to be creative at home.
- It will mean *learning to value all that God has made* – the world he has created and the people he has put in it. When we take care of God's world, we are doing what God intended. Similarly, to value other people and care for the poor and needy shows that we love God. The Bible records that Jesus said, 'I tell you the truth, whatever you did for one of the least of these brothers of mine, you did for me' (Matthew 25:40). When we make a sandwich for one of the homeless people who regularly come to our door, we often try to let the children take part, telling them what God says about caring for the poor.
- It will mean *reminding our children constantly that all the gifts they have come from God*. If your child talks of becoming a teacher, for example, you could point out that one day he might be able to teach in a church children's group – as a way of being thankful for the teaching gift God has given him.

Finally, here are some ideas about what you – as a family – might do to show that you value others, especially those less fortunate than yourselves.

- Sponsor a child in a developing country, for example through the Toybox Charity.[1]
- Raise money for a project that helps the homeless.
- Give clothes and toys to others more needy than your own family.
- At Christmas take part in a project that gives toys to children who otherwise would not have any, for example through the Samaritans Purse Organization.[2]

Many of the things we have mentioned here will not come naturally! We will need to work at it, but it is our firm belief that, as we gently and prayerfully teach and encourage our children to love God, it will gradually become a way of life for them.

2. Our children's relationship with Mum and Dad

Our relationship with our children is obviously very important, and we can keep that relationship healthy by teaching our children that it is good to respect Mum and Dad. Of course, respect comes from the heart and will grow out of our relationship with them, but we can teach them gently but firmly how to respect us in practical ways.

The most important element of our children's relationship with us will be love, and with that needs to come lots of fun and laughter together. When we talk about respecting Mum and Dad, we are not advocating a return to the Victorian era when children were seen and not heard – and we are sure that was not what God meant either (see Exodus 20). It is so important to enjoy an open, warm relationship with our children in which they can come to us at any time, with anything on their hearts, and know that we who love them unconditionally will always accept them and will do all we can to sort out what is troubling them. It is quite possible for all of this to go hand in hand with an attitude of respect. In fact, our children are much more likely to come to us in this way if they have grown up to respect us and value our opinions.

What can we do, then, to help our children to live out this attitude of respect?

We should be wary of trying to be friends with our children from day one. This may go against our initial desire, because we all want to be accepted by our children and to be 'friends' brings real security. To be a parent is a privilege, however, so let's be just that. To seek to be friends confuses our children and implies an equal relationship, which is not possible when you consider all the responsibility that we have as parents.

Friendship is our ultimate goal in adulthood, and we reach it gradually.

This may be more difficult if you are parenting on your own, because you may be tempted to share your problems with your child and perhaps to allow your child to fill a gap in your life (see Chapter 2). Letting our children be equals may satisfy a short-term need, but in the end, when they are older, they may lose respect for our authority and standards and may even reject the relationship they have with us.

We can also help our children to respect us by *teaching them to be careful how they speak to us and by correcting them if they are rude*. Sometimes it will come as a complete revelation to them that they were being rude in the way they acted or spoke. Just because we adults recognize rudeness does not mean that our children will, so we should take care to point it out gently.

When our children are very young – under the age of three – our parenting will be typified by lots of 'nos' and 'don'ts' (see Chapter 6). They simply will not understand the reason why they should not shout at us or say 'no' to us. If your child is at that stage and speaks rudely to you, you could say firmly, 'You mustn't speak to me like that!' or, 'You don't say "no" to Mum!' If this sort of rudeness continues, it might be appropriate to correct it in some other way.

As they grow past the age of three or four, we should aim to help our children move from not being rude to Mum or Dad because they might be made to sit on the stairs, to respecting us out of love and actively desiring to treat us with respect. For our older children, then, it should be enough simply to explain, 'The way you spoke to me then wasn't respectful.' As children who do want to respect us, they will probably not speak in that way again.

Here are some ideas for practical things we can do to encourage our children to respect us.

- Have Mum and Dad sit at the head of the table at family mealtimes.
- Have Mum and Dad sit in the front seats of the car.
- Have younger children ask before taking a drink or a biscuit and before using the telephone.

For our children, their relationship with their parents has a very important part to play in teaching them to look outward, away from themselves. It is the closest relationship they have, certainly in the very early years, and it should be the one in which they feel most secure. It is therefore a safe place from which to learn the attributes of respect and putting others first. With a little thought and effort on our part, we can make it very easy for our children to live this out.

3. Our children's relationship with their brothers and sisters

There is nothing quite like having a brother or sister to play with, to share laughs with, to share tears with, to share toys with, and to help you learn to put others before yourself by sharing Mum and Dad's hugs and Grandpa and Grandma's sweets, by taking turns, by letting someone else have their drink in the Disney cup you had rather been hoping to use yourself! Clearly, because people matter, brothers and sisters matter, and we can work at seeing our children put each other first (see Romans 12:10). Also, our children's relationship with a sibling is often the first peer relationship they form. If they can learn how to treat their siblings, it will make other peer relationships so much easier later on.

What can we do to help our children value their brothers and sisters, and to demonstrate that people matter in this very special family relationship?

- Try referring to your children's siblings as 'your brother' or 'your sister' as a change from calling them by their Christian name. This is a good way of reinforcing the relationship for them and helping them to know what a special thing it is. Also you could say things like, 'Isn't it lovely that N is your brother/sister?' This serves to *remind them that a brother or sister is great to have* – someone with whom they will always be the best of friends and therefore need to take care of.

- *When one of them is being kind to the other, try to praise them for it.* This brings to their attention the fact that what they did was to think of others rather than themselves, and it will encourage them, having received praise for it, to do it again next time.

- Try to *encourage them to be glad when something good happens to one of their siblings*, and praise them when they manage it.

- Squabbles between brothers and sisters are inevitable, but they need not get out of hand. It is sad to hear brothers and sisters calling each other names or putting each other down. There is a proverb that says, 'Reckless words pierce like a sword, but the tongue of the wise brings healing' (Proverbs 12:18). We should not underestimate the harm that can be done if a child is constantly put down by a sibling. Equally, we should not underestimate the good that can come from the carefully chosen words of a loving brother or sister. *Encourage your children to be sensitive to one another's feelings.* Teach them how to listen and respond to one another in a way that will build each other up.

- *Encourage your children to be aware of the good qualities that their brothers and sisters have.* Periodically during family time, ask the children what they especially like about each of the others. This not only reinforces in our children positive feelings towards their siblings, but also encourages each of them as they learn of qualities they perhaps did not know they had.

Children who are fortunate enough to have brothers and sisters have a wonderful opportunity for learning how to put others first and how to let them feel valued.

4. Our children's relationship with other adults

Children are very honest, and what we see in their outward behaviour is often a reflection of what is in their heart. It is therefore all the more uplifting to be spoken to by a child who is happy to talk and has learned how to value adults in spite of the difference in age. Obviously there are times when children will say the wrong thing in childish innocence, and everyone forgives them for it. Nonetheless, there are also things that we can actively teach them, which will help them to make other adults feel respected and valued. Simple things such as giving up their seat for an older person or holding the door open for others will, if we teach them to our children, help them to look outward through the way they relate to other adults.

What else can we do to help our children demonstrate respect for other adults?

- *Devise some family guidelines for your children about what to do when an adult speaks to them.* Shyness is very common among young children, but they will feel much more confident if they have prior preparation about what to do and say. You could encourage your children to look an adult in the eye, say 'hello' and respond to any questions briefly. It is amazing what a difference it makes to a child's approach to an adult once they know what to do and say, and why they should act in that way.

- *Teach your children how to get your attention in an appropriate way* when you are in conversation with another adult. You could teach them to come and place their hand on your arm or waist when they need to tell you something, and to wait patiently. You can then place your hand on theirs to let them know you are aware of them and are waiting for a suitable break in the conversation to attend to them. Then you can ask them what they want. This lets everyone know, including your children, that other people matter and that you want to demonstrate this. It also allows your children to communicate their needs to you, knowing they can trust you to meet them.

- *Encourage your children from an early age to write thank-you letters for the presents they receive*, as a means of demonstrating an awareness of the preciousness of others. For the very young ones, you could write the letters yourself, but from four or five they can easily dictate what they want to say. At six they could write one letter to photocopy and perhaps fill in the names and items, and from about seven or eight they could probably manage to write most of their letters themselves.

- *When you go to a public place* such as a library or doctor's surgery, or to certain church services where people particularly need peace and quiet, you could remind the children of that before you arrive.

- *Mealtimes are always a great opportunity for thinking of others*. Encourage your children to use good manners by not starting until everyone is served, by saying 'please' and 'thank you', by eating with their mouth closed, and by complimenting the cook. These are all ways of showing that they are thinking of those at the table, guests and family alike. Even babies can use good manners. You could teach your baby sign language so that he can say 'please' and 'thank you' and 'more, please' and 'drink, please' before he can speak (babies can often pick this up from about a year, sometimes earlier). It makes for much more peaceful family mealtimes!

5. Our children's relationship with their friends

What can we do, in this age of competition, to encourage our children to value their friends and peers?

- *We can help them to be glad when something good happens to one of their friends.* Every week on a Friday afternoon at our children's school, a shield is given out to the pupil who has been the kindest or friendliest to others during that week. One day I overheard one of the boys excitedly telling his mother that his friend had won the shield that day. She replied, 'Oh, that's wonderful! And did you all give him a clap?' It was such a simple thing to say, but it struck me then that she was encouraging him to be glad for his friend and cheer him on. That shield has a very special place in the life of the school, and we are thankful for that.

- *Encourage them to respect their friends' belongings* and, at other people's houses, to wait until they are invited to play with the toys, or at least to ask before they dive in. There is much in the Bible about ownership of property, and we can teach this to our children in relation to their friends' possessions, and also those of their siblings. You could also help your children to understand the value of belongings and property by encouraging them to do little jobs to earn money, such as tidying up any litter in the front garden, dusting and polishing, and cleaning windows. These are extra jobs, not the usual household chores which everyone helps with. It is a great way for them to save up for something they want to buy, and will help to teach them the value of things because they have to work for them.

- *Encourage them to look out for children who might be on their own* in the playground and to include them in their games.

- To the moan of 'It's not fair', which every parent must hear many times, *explain to the children that life is not always fair*, and help them to remember and be thankful for what they have rather than what they do not have. Help them to see that to think of what we do not have is to focus on ourselves and will only make us discontented.

- *Encourage them to pray for their friends* – not just generally, but for specific needs. Nothing will boost their faith more than for God to answer prayers for their friends.

- *Encourage them to feel very privileged when they receive an invitation to a party*. Remind them what a privilege it is to be counted as someone's friend.

Here are some ideas about how you can reinforce the idea of a party invitation from a friend being something special.

- Encourage them to make their own wrapping paper by colouring blank sheets of paper.

- Encourage them to make their own birthday card to give to their friend.
- Let them choose and wrap the present with you.
- Have them pay a bit towards the present when they are old enough.

Setting an example

There is one final thing to say before we close this chapter. We have been concentrating on the ways in which we can teach our children how to show that other people matter. It is essential that we also teach by our own example. Our children will be watching us to see whether we live out what we teach. We might ask ourselves how we treat our husband or wife, our close family, our friends and other adults. Do we speak positively about them when they are not there? Do we encourage them and actively do things to show that we value them?

In the early years, our children learn more from copying what we do than we realize.

We have an opportunity to bring up our children to care for those around them and to do the right thing in terms of their relationships with others. To adopt this lifestyle will be helpful not only for our own families, but also for the communities in which we live.

Taking it further

1. Spot your child being kind to a sibling or friend without being prompted, and give him or her lots of praise.
2. Teach your children how to get your attention when you are talking to another person, and see how long it takes for them to catch on.

10

Keeping the Vision in Mind

Over the last nine chapters we have tried in different ways to encourage you to dream big dreams for your family – to have a vision for your family and to believe that it is possible for that vision to become a reality, with God's help.

So often in life we have dreams. We dream, perhaps, of one day flying an aeroplane, or of driving in a racing car round the Silverstone race track, or of playing in the final at Wimbledon, or perhaps simply of making a significant difference in this world in some way. Sometimes these dreams become a reality; sometimes they do not. We hope that as you have read this book you have built up a dream for your family which you now believe it is possible to achieve. This dream will not be just another good idea which came to nothing. Our prayer is that you have been inspired to make changes, to do things differently, to be proactive in making your family life even more fulfilling and pleasurable than it has been so far. Our hope is that you have dreams, goals and aims for your family now which you did not have before you began.

The thing about dreams is that you have to hold on to

them. More often than not, you have to work at making them come true. In this last chapter we want to encourage you not to let go of your dream, but to work at it until you see it come true. What, then, can we do to help ourselves? The Bible talks in several places of the triad of faith, hope and love, three key qualities in our Christian walk. We want to suggest that these three qualities are just as key in holding on to our dreams and visions for our families.

Faith

God is faithful, and we can trust him to take care of every aspect of our family life if we entrust it to him. He will honour those families who seek to honour him. As we prayerfully commit our ways to him, he will watch over us and guide us in our family life.

Our own faith in God is central to all that we do as parents, and we have an opportunity to pass that faith on to our children. We can teach our children about God and his ways, but at the end of the day it will be our actions that will make the difference. Where our words are matched by life and action, they will sink in.

Central to our Christian faith is the fact that through Jesus we have forgiveness for our sins. This will be a reality to our children if they see it lived out in us. Sometimes, therefore, we may need to say 'sorry' to our children when we get it wrong. We have to model what we are saying. If we expect our children to say 'sorry' to each other, then it is important for them to hear Mum and Dad saying 'sorry' to one another too, and to know that we will say 'sorry' to them when we get things wrong.

God has given us the Bible to help us in our parenting, and we will need to have faith in it. We will always be bombarded with advice on different ways of parenting and new ideas that might or might not work. Of course we should listen and weigh up the collective thoughts of the 'experts', but we can also have faith in what God has given us and not allow ourselves to be blown this way and that by the latest idea.

Have faith that with God's help you can build a better marriage. You may already have a good marriage, but there is always something you can do to make it better. Buy each other a book on marriage for a birthday or Christmas present and read it together. Reading new material and listening to other people's advice is always helpful, even if we do not always agree with it, because it makes us more committed to the life we have chosen to lead.

Here are some actions you might take to help you invest in your marriage.

- Take time for each other.
- Look for the good and the beautiful in each other.
- Stand together with a mutual sense of values and a common objective.
- Speak words of appreciation.
- Find things to praise in each other.
- Always have the capacity to forgive and forget.
- Do not be a historical partner – one who always digs up the past – because you can bury a marriage with a lot of little digs.
- Look to the future, think how you would like it to be, and then go for it.

Often in life, things are what we make them, and if we invest in our marriages then we will have the best marriages on earth. Try to have a 'honeymoon' every year, even if it is only for 24 hours. To take time away from the children and invest in the most important relationship in the home is crucial if we are to stay fresh and together in our parenting.

It is not just about marrying the right partner, but about *being* the right partner.

Our marriages are what we want them to be. We have quite a large garden at home and every now and then we will spend a couple of days digging the flowerbeds, trimming the bushes and cutting the grass, and the garden looks great. It looks great because we have invested in it. Yet it does not take long for the weeds to grow back, the grass to grow long and the bushes to look messy again. The same is true of our marriages. We have to do a little each day, to ensure that we live in love and peace together. If we invest in them, then the return will be great.

Have faith to believe that you are God's appointed parents for your children. Your children want to belong to your family. There could not be a better Mum and Dad for them. God intended that you bring up your children. They love you as Mum and Dad more than anyone else. You are the best parents that they could ever have hoped for. To them you are the greatest. Build on this faith that they have in you. Do not give up working at your family identity. Work at ways of building on those God-given relationships.

Have faith in your values. We live in a feel-good world today, and many of your values may well go against the majority view. Nonetheless, believe that your values are good and try your hardest to stick to them. As we place the biblical values of honesty and respect in our children's hearts, and as we live them out in our own lives, so we will build a better tomorrow for our children's children.

Have faith in your methods of discipline. Consistency is so important. There will be people who do not agree with your way of parenting, but there will be many others who do. Do not be tempted to conform to other people's views. You are the best parent for your child. Have faith in that. It is OK to say 'no' to our children. It is OK to expect them to think of others. It is better for them to know what is acceptable and what is not, because then they have great freedom within the boundaries we have set. Discipline helps our children to enjoy life.

Have faith in God that he has heard your prayers for your children. One of the hardest things that a parent is called to do is to let go. It starts happening as a child begins to go to school, then it builds over the childhood years, until at some point the child leaves home. One of the most important aspects of letting go is to trust God for your child. Of course, our praying never stops and we never stop being parents. However, our role changes to that of a spectator as we watch our children find their own way in life.

Hope

Hope is a great thing. It allows us to stand firm in what we believe, even when things around us seem grim. There will be times when we, as families, go through hard times. No one escapes those. Everyone has difficulties of some sort – a bereavement in the family, a child being bullied at school, a teenager going through a lonely time, a redundancy, a marriage break-up. Very few people go through life without experiencing some kind of trouble. The important thing is never to lose hope. Know that with God there is always a brighter future ahead, and he will always help us through the darkest of times. Hope is an integral part of being a parent. As parents we *need* hope.

- We hope that our children have caught our values.
- We hope that they will find a mission in life.
- We hope that when our children are small we have instilled in them a sense of purpose, a thirst to make the best of all things, and a desire to make a difference in this world.

Hope is wonderful.
It always looks forward to good things.

The question 'What do you want to do when you grow up?' is so much more rewarding when it concerns not just economic activities but values, character and the contribution that your child hopes to make to the future shape of this world.

So we place into our children's hearts our values and beliefs. We place into their lives good things that will build them up and give them the best start possible. We pray for them and share with them our dreams for a better world and more loving communities. We hope that by the time they leave home they too will be committed to changing the world. We hope that they will be committed to bringing up their children following God's guidelines.

Love

Our children need to know our unconditional love. This will mean laughing, playing and having fun and adventures together. It will mean pouring onto our children our unconditional love – a love that is accepting yet guiding.

We live in a varied and diverse world. Our children face a noisy, image-conscious, information-soaked, complex, over-stimulating world full of challenges, opportunities and choices. What we are seeking to provide at home is *a place of security and love* – a place where they know they will always be loved and looked after; a place where they can just be who God has called them to be; a place where they are allowed to fail as well as succeed. This is the value that holds this book together: the value of love.

- Love does not demand performance and always offers forgiveness.
- Love should seek to build up and guide in right ways.
- Love should not be afraid to discipline for a better end.

Parenting is such an exciting calling. It is the highest calling we can have. God has entrusted us with lives to mould and shape. Into these lives we can place the unconditional love of God as well as our own unconditional love.

This is a love that will commit you to start praying for your family. The testimony of many people who have followed our course is that it has inspired them to start praying for their children and their children's future partners, if marriage is something to which God calls them. In faith we have this great and certain hope that God will hear our prayers and answer them. As we pray, so our children will pray.

It is also a love that will commit you to make time to be with your children. We are all faced with choices in life about how we spend our time and money. We urge you to choose, when it is possible, to get home from work in time to see your children. We urge you to make time to spend with the children doing things together at weekends. Memories are made from these moments.

With faith, hope and love, in large quantities, our dreams for our families can come true. They really are within our grasp. The exciting thing is that, as we work at making our dreams a reality, we will impact not only our immediate families but also the communities in which we live, the churches to which we belong and the schools our children attend. If we walk the talk of good parenting, if we live it out, then our children will catch it from us. If we provide for our children a model for parenting that is based on the Bible and that gives them a happy, secure childhood, and yet also prepares them for tomorrow's world, then they will (we hope) do the same for their children. In addition, as others see what we are doing and begin to dream their own dreams and work at seeing them come true, we really will be making a difference to the society in which we live. We really will be doing something to make this world a better place.

Let's return now to where we began in Chapter 1. We talked about how helpful it is to have a destination in mind for our family, to know where we want to get to. Without that destination in mind, we can end up moving from vision to survival. Our original hopes and dreams for our family get lost because everyday management seems so overwhelming. We hope that over these ten chapters you have been reminded of your original hopes and dreams. Maybe you have also been inspired to dream new dreams. We hope that you are excited by the vision you now have for your family.

Creating a family vision statement

We would like to encourage you to put together your own family vision statement. You can all agree it together (or agree it as parents at this stage, and review it as the children get older) and perhaps put it up in a prominent place to remind you of the things that are important to you as a family. It will give the family a fixed point of reference. You can look at it from time to time and ask yourselves the following questions.

- How are we doing as a family?
- Are we living out the things we consider to be important?
- Are we spending time together?
- How are we treating each other?
- Are we being encouraging?
- Are we giving as well as taking?
- Are we thinking of those outside the family as well as ourselves?
- Is our home a place of peace and harmony, a place to which we all enjoy coming back?
- Are we living as God would have us live?

Step 1

Either at family time or round the family meal table, introduce the idea of having a family vision statement. Explain what it is and see what people think of the idea. Do not push it! If there is little interest, leave it until another time. Unless everyone owns it, they will not be committed to it. If they seem excited by the idea, go on to Step 2.

Step 2

Explain that at the next family time, or some other appointed time, you can all start to put the vision statement together. You might suggest that it could include the following things:

- What kind of family do we want to be?
- What kind of atmosphere do we want in our home?
- How do we want to treat each other and speak to one another?
- What are the responsibilities of each family member?
- What things are important to us as a family?
- What guidelines do we want to live by?
- How do we want to treat other people?
- What is the purpose of our family?
- How can we make a difference to the community in which we live?

Make it clear that each member will have an opportunity to say what they think is important. Encourage each family member to go off and think carefully about what they want to be included in the family vision statement.

Step 3

At the appointed time, come back together with a piece of paper and begin to discuss your vision statement. Go round the family and take turns to say the things you feel are important. Discuss them as you go, and write them down. You will need some ground rules:

- Everyone listens when someone is speaking.
- Everyone respects what others say.
- Everyone has a chance to say everything they want to say.

Step 4

Once you have a draft, leave it for a while so that people can think about it, revisit it, and agree changes if necessary.

Step 5

Once everyone is happy with the vision statement, create the final document, have everyone sign it and date it, and then display it in the place where you most often gather as a family. Use it to keep your destination in mind.

Step 6

Review your vision statement every year.

Below, to give you some ideas, is an example of a vision statement created by one family who followed the Family Time course (reproduced with their permission).

Things that are important to our family

1. All of us are to tell the truth.
2. First time obedience to Mum and Dad.
3. Mum and Dad not to aggravate the children.
4. Stealing is always wrong. When we borrow things – we will look after them as if they were our own and not be jealous.
5. We will support and encourage each other, especially when we get things wrong.
6. We will listen to each other.
7. We will show kindness to each other by sharing our own things and time e.g. by helping around the house.
8. Remember: people are more important than things.
9. It's important to have fun and laughter together as a family.
10. We love God and want to serve him.

Conclusion

Our aims in this book have been many. Perhaps, however, the greatest aim has been to produce something that is as practical as possible. We have attempted to provide a model for parenting which we have found helpful and which is based in the Bible. We hope that you will take what you can from it and apply it to your life and the lives of your children.

We hope you have seen that the Bible has a great deal to say about parenting and that there is so much we can do ourselves to make family life fun and rewarding. We hope also that you will have seen that much of what we have been teaching on parenting relates to our relationship with God. This means that our own spiritual growth is not at odds with our parenting, but will enhance it and be in harmony with it.

Our role as parents will not always be an easy one – and the fact that you have read a book about it does not mean that family life will henceforth be problem-free! Nonetheless, we do hope that we have encouraged you to find a fresh vision for your family. And we pray that all we have discussed will do for you and your children what it has done for us and ours.

* * *

If children live with criticism they learn to condemn.

If children live with hostility they learn to fight.

If children live with ridicule they learn to be shy.

If children live with shame they learn to feel guilty.

If children live with tolerance they learn to be patient.

If children live with encouragement they learn confidence.

If children live with appreciation they learn to appreciate.

If children live with fairness they learn justice.

If children live with security they learn to have faith.

If children live with approval they learn to like themselves.

If children live with acceptance and friendship they learn to find love.

Appendix 1

How to Run a Family Time Course

To help you run a course in your own church or school, here are some of the things that we find help the course to run smoothly and successfully at St Paul's.

How long does it last?

The course involves ten sessions which can be run in consecutive weeks. Alternatively, we have found that it also works well to have the sessions every other week. The most important thing is to find out what would best suit your community and the child-care provision needed for your group.

Who should take part?

Ideally, if both parents are together, the couple should do the course together. We have tried it both ways and the results are far more positive if both parents have taken part. Like us, you might think at first that this will put people off – especially if their husband or wife is not keen to do the course with them. We have found, however, that as we have

persevered in encouraging couples to come together, the
partner who was perhaps less keen initially has become
committed and been glad that he or she signed up!

Obviously, those parenting on their own are also encouraged to attend and welcomed with open arms. It is helpful
to put them in groups with others who are parenting alone,
but not exclusively.

Who should speak and lead?

To lead a Family Time course, you will be someone who is
seeking to learn all you can about parenting and interested
not only in sharing those lessons with others but also in
learning from others. Everyone who attends a course has
something valuable to add and we all continue to learn,
however many children we have or whatever our experience
has been.

You will need to have a bit of experience of family life, so
you will not be brand-new parents, and ideally you will
have children of various ages, the oldest one preferably
older than or of a similar age to those of other parents on
the course. We encourage those parenting alone to share the
leading of the course.

It is a good idea to use some appropriate jokes or e-mails
at the start of your talks. Laughter is a great tension-releaser
and enables people to relax.

What is the format of a typical evening?

We begin at 8 p.m. with a welcome and notices, and then
we go straight into the talk. During the talk, people are

encouraged to make notes in their Family Time Handbooks.

It is helpful if those who are speaking can use their own examples of family life as they present the material, but feel free to use any example from the book.

After the talk we offer refreshments (tea and coffee with cakes, which course participants bring on a rota basis each week). This social time is crucial and usually lasts about twenty minutes. It is a great opportunity for people to get to know one another and to share stories. After that we split into groups. It is helpful to choose group leaders who will facilitate the discussion.

How many are in a group?

Ideally we would have between ten and twelve people in a group. This gives plenty of opportunity to hear about others' experiences, and is not so large that it intimidates people from participating in free discussion.

What happens in the groups?

In Session 1 we would begin by asking the group to introduce themselves, covering the following points:

- Names and ages of children
- Length of marriage if applicable
- Occupation/interests
- Church/organizations
- What each person hopes to gain from the course for them and their family

Thereafter we begin each group session with a recap on the previous week, seeing if anyone has used the points given under 'Taking it further' and discussing any questions that have arisen. Then we have an open discussion following on from the talk we have just heard.

There are suggested questions in Appendix 2, following these notes, but we would encourage you to be flexible and use them simply as a means of drawing out the themes from the talk. You might want to start by simply asking, 'What struck you in the talk this evening?' or, 'What was the most important thing for you in tonight's talk?'

During the discussion groups, do not feel at any time that you have to do all the talking as group leader. Our experience is that by Session 3 you will have to say very little, because everybody on the course has something to share by then. Also, do not be afraid to leave silences. Often people are preparing to say something, and if we break the silence they may have lost that opportunity.

We close with prayer if appropriate (we usually ask for requests from the families in the group), and this might be either open prayer or one of the leaders praying for everything, depending on the group make-up. It may be that some groups do not start praying until Session 4 or 5 (by which time the material has already talked about praying for your children), but we would encourage you to pray in your groups at some point in the course. Once prayer has been introduced, then pray each time!

Timing

It is important to start and end on time, particularly because the very nature of the course means that people will need to get home to relieve babysitters. Running each session from 8 to 10 p.m. works well.

Babysitting

It is a good idea, when writing to each participant with details of the course, to include the telephone number of the Family Time venue. Parents need to be contactable and it will inspire confidence if they know you have thought of it ahead of time. It is worth saying, too, that in our church we have a Babysitting Ministry which has been set up especially to cater for courses such as Family Time and Alpha. A lack of babysitters can be a real hindrance to parents doing the course and if we can cross that hurdle for them, it may well be the deciding factor as to whether they come or not.

Photos

About halfway through the course, we encourage everyone to bring in photos of their children. By this time people have got to know one another and they enjoy seeing pictures of the children they have been hearing about.

Ongoing support

We believe it is important for people to be supported as they seek to continue to work on their family life once the course is over. We do try to encourage couples to link up and support one another, and this often happens very naturally as people have made new friends through doing the course together. In addition, we arrange a reunion about three months after the course has finished. We have tended either to take over a local restaurant for an evening, or to have a meal in someone's home to which everyone brings a contribution of food. It is a great evening, full of good food and a lot of fun.

Resources

Our desire is that you will take the course material and adapt it to suit your own situation. You can do this by taking each chapter in the book and presenting it as a session.

Alternatively, to help you put your talks together, a set of talk manuscripts can be bought electronically by visiting *www.newwinedirect.co.uk*, or by contacting Kingsway on *books@kingsway.co.uk*. These talks can then be used as a resource to cut and paste on your own computer, so that you can insert your own examples of family life and present the material yourself.

A set of audio-tapes can also be bought from New Wine Trust by phoning 020 8799 3778, or e-mailing *info@new-wine.org*, or writing to New Wine, 4a Ridley Avenue, Ealing, London, W13 9XW.

Cost

It is a good idea to make a nominal charge for doing the course, as this tends to give people a sense of ownership and also enables you to provide members with the *Family Time Handbook* and coffee at no extra charge. We would suggest a charge of between £5 and £10 per couple/individual.

Bookstall

You might like to have a bookstall out, if not every week, at least during some of the sessions, selling some of the recommended reading titles and any others you have found helpful.

We would encourage you to have copies of *Family Time* available for everyone doing the course, because people will find it helpful to read through the book as the course progresses.

Session 5, because of the nature of the material, is a good time to have a full bookstall out, with all the recommended reading plus children's Bibles, Bible reading notes and other Christian books and videos. A local Christian bookshop will normally supply these on a sale or return basis.

We hope these suggestions are all helpful and will give you the confidence to run your own Family Time course. For more details or help in running a Family Time Course, call 020 8799 3778 or e-mail *mark.melluish@new-wine.org*.

Appendix 2

Suggested Questions for Discussion Groups

Session 1: A Vision for the Family

1. What was the most important thing for you in this evening's talk?
2. What are your dreams for your family? Do you have a picture of how you would like it to be in an ideal world?
3. Are you attracted by the idea of focusing on our children's hearts rather than on their behaviour?
4. Can you see how explaining the reason why when you ask your child to do something would be more likely to get a positive response?
5. 'Children may not be very good at listening to their elders, but they nearly always seem to find ways of imitating them.' How do you respond to this statement?

Recommended reading for this session

Mark and Lindsay Melluish, *Family Time*, Kingsway Publications, 2002

Session 2: Love and Marriage

1. 'The most important thing a father can do for his children is to love their mother.' How do you respond to this statement?
2. Think back to your own childhood. Did everything revolve around the children, or was equal attention given to all family members?
3. In what ways do you think revolving everything solely around the children could be detrimental to the family as a whole?
4. Gary Chapman in *The Five Love Languages* says that love is a choice. What do you think he means?
5. Do you relate personally to the suggestion that certain acts make you feel loved more than others?

Recommended reading for this session

Gary Chapman, *The Five Love Languages*, Northfield Publishing, 1995

John and Anne Coles, *Making More of Marriage*, New Wine International, 2000

Willard F. Harley, *His Needs, Her Needs*, Fleming H. Revell Co., 1995

Nicky and Sila Lee, *The Marriage Book*, HTB Publications London, 2000

Rob Parsons, *Loving Against the Odds*, Hodder & Stoughton, 1998

Session 3: When They Are Young

1. How good are you at hearing what other people are saying?

2. Think back to your childhood. What was communication like in your family? Did you feel listened to as a child?

3. In what ways have you already sought to encourage your children to express themselves?

4. Can you share your own ideas about how you have spent time with your children and invested in relationship-building?

Recommended reading for this session

Gary Chapman and Ross Campbell, *The Five Love Languages for Children*, Northfield Publishing, 1995

Adele Faber and Elaine Maglish, *How to Talk so Kids Will Listen and Listen so Kids Will Talk*, Avon Books, 2002

Rob Parsons, *The Sixty Minute Father*, Hodder & Stoughton, 1995

Session 4: Family Time

1. Family circumstances play an important role in children's lives. Talk, if you can, about your circumstances. How do you think these things have affected your children?

2. Can you share anything from your own childhood experiences? Are you aware of things you grew up with that have had a positive or negative effect on you?

3. Did you grow up in a family with a strong identity? If so, what made it strong?

4. What about our families now? Can we see strong identities developing, or are there steps we could take to strengthen them?

Session 5: Outside Influences

1. Who or what had the greatest influence on you when you were a child, besides your family? Was this a good thing or not?
2. What are your thoughts about the influence that TV, computers, friends, etc. can have on your child?
3. One of the aims of this course is to help equip your child to cope with these influences. Do you think that this is possible?
4. We have heard that a personal relationship with Jesus makes a difference in the way our children respond to their influences. Was this true for you as a child, and if so, how do you feel it made a difference for you? Is it true for your children now, and if so, can you share ways in which you have sought to encourage them in their relationship with God?

Recommended reading for this session

Stormie Omartian, *Power of a Praying Parent*, Kingsway Publications, 1996
Various children's books and Bibles

Session 6: Transmitting Values

1. Are you aware of values you grew up with, either positive or negative? What part do they play in adult life?
2. What values are we putting into our children's hearts, and how are we doing that?
3. Think about your own conscience. Is it healthy? Are you someone who responds from guilt or because

it is the right thing to do?

4. How does it encourage you to know that we can empower our children now and for adult life by helping to shape their conscience while they are young?

Recommended reading for this session

J John, *Ten*, Kingsway Publications, 2000

Session 7: Training and Obedience

1. As a child, how were you expected to respond to your parents' requests? Was obedience a part of life in your childhood home?

2. What is our response now when we are required to obey the law, for example? Do we do it willingly?

3. Do you relate to parents who threaten, repeat themselves, bribe, negotiate in conflict or allow too much choice? What are your experiences?

4. Children often rise to the level of their parents' expectation. What is your response to this?

5. What are your thoughts on the subject of obedience? Is it part of your experience, and if not, do you see it as an achievable or desirable thing?

6. God has given us the joy and responsibility of disciplining our children. How do you respond to this?

Session 8: Taking Corrective Action

1. What was your experience of being disciplined as a child? Has this affected your approach now as a parent?

2. How do you respond to the idea of discipline being more than punishment?

3. What are your thoughts about the different stages of correction for deliberate naughtiness? How could you see them helping you in the future, if they have not already?

4. How do you respond to the ideas on repenting, forgiving and making amends? How might this work out in your family?

Session 9: Modelling Love and Respect

1. Consider the relationship you have with your parents and ask, 'Is this as I would want it to be with my children when they are my age?'

2. How easily do you feel glad when something good happens to someone else?

3. Do you live your life, and encourage your children to live their lives, in a way that demonstrates the family value that 'other people matter'? How successful are you in this?

4. How successful have you been in encouraging healthy relationships between siblings?

Session 10: Keeping the Vision in Mind

1. What is the most significant thing about this course for you and your family?

2. Do you have a fresh vision for your family now that the course is ending? If so, could you share it?

3. Are there things that you as a family have put into place during the course which have encouraged you? What are they?

Notes

Chapter 1

1. Stephen Covey, *The Seven Habits of Highly Effective Families* (Simon & Schuster Ltd, 1998).
2. Bill Hybels, *Honest to God* (Zondervan, 1992).

Chapter 2

1. Willard F. Harley, *His Needs, Her Needs* (Fleming H. Revell Co., 1995).
2. John Gray, *Men are from Mars, Women are from Venus* (Harper Collins, 1992).
3. Gary Chapman, *The Five Love Languages* (Northfield Publishing, 1995).

Chapter 3

1. 'What is a Grandma?', submitted by Nurse Juanita Nelson, appeared in the employee newspaper at Children's Hospital, Los Angeles.

2. Ted Tripp, *Shepherding a Child's Heart* (Shepherd Press, 1995).

3. Paul Planet, *Let's Hug, Once upon a Planet* (Bay Side, New York, 1981).

4. Wayne Rice, *Hot Illustrations for Youth Talks* (Zondervan, 1995).

Chapter 6

The second part of this chapter is based on ideas from *Growing Kids God's Way* by Gary and Anne-Marie Ezzo (Growing Families Int. 1993).

Chapter 8

1. Rob Parsons, *The Sixty-Minute Father* (Hodder & Stoughton, 1995).

2. Steve Chalke, *How to Succeed as a Parent* (Hodder & Stoughton, 1997).

Chapter 9

1. The Toybox Charity (Helping Street Children in Guatemala) is contactable at: PO Box 660, Amersham, Bucks HP6 6EA; e-mail: *info@toybox.org*; website: *www.toybox.org*.

2. The Samaritans Purse Organization (working with children in the Eastern Bloc) is contactable at: Samaritans Purse Int. Ltd, Victoria House, Victoria Road, Buckhurst Hill, Essex IG9 5EX; e-mail: *info@samaritans-purse.org.uk*.

Family Time – The Course Handbook

by Lindsay and Mark Melluish

If you want to run the Family Time course in your own church situation, this handbook is an essential tool for course members and leaders to use alongside the main book.

The ten sessions are all covered, including exercises to complete, questions for 'taking it further' and recommended reading suggestions.

Kingsway Publications

Praying the Bible with Your Family

by David and Heather Kopp

Designed to capture the children's interest as well as inspire and challenge mum and dad, this latest book in the *Praying the Bible* series is fun-packed, story-oriented and a practical devotional tool. It will help every parent and child to have a healthy, growing, Bible-based prayer life.

Includes key scriptures, devotional text, Bible trivia, prayers for special occasions and more.

DAVID KOPP is the founding editor of *Christian Parenting Today*. HEATHER is a writer and editor. David remembers his father 'praying the Bible' for him, a legacy he and Heather continue with their own family.

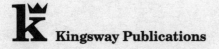 **Kingsway Publications**